LEADERSHIP IS MALE

LEADERSHIP IS MALE

A Division of Thomas Nelson Publishers
Nashville

First published in the United Kingdom by Highland Books, 1988, 1989. This edition published in Nashville, Tennessee, by Oliver-Nelson Books, a division of Thomas Nelson, Inc., Publishers, and distributed in Canada by Lawson Falle, Ltd., Cambridge, Ontario.

Scripture quotations are taken from the HOLY BIBLE: NEW INTERNATIONAL VERSION. Copyright © 1973, 1978, 1984 by the International Bible Society. Used by permission of Zondervan Bible Publishers.

Scripture quotations noted KJV are from The King James Version of the Holy Bible.

Library of Congress Cataloging-in-Publication Data

Pawson, J. David.
    Leadership is male / J. David Pawson.
        p.   cm.
    ISBN 0-8407-9023-6
    1. Patriarchy—Biblical teaching.   2. Leadership—Biblical
teaching.   3. Sex role—Biblical teaching.   I. Title.
BS680.P36P38   1990
262'.1—dc20   89-71033
                                                                CIP

Printed in the United States of America.
1 2 3 4 5 6 — 95 94 93 92 91 90

CONTENTS

94566

LEADERSHIP
IS
MALE

FOREWORD

What a relief to find a bold book with a bold title on a subject most men won't touch with a barge pole! I don't know Mr. Pawson, but surely he is a bold man. He faced the cost of putting his "obsolete and offensive" (his own words) viewpoint into print and went ahead and did it anyway—with scholarly care, with grace and courtesy. I hope and pray that people will read and heed what he has written.

The issue of so-called equality of men and women touches the very foundation of Christian faith, for it goes deep into the nature of God and the great mystery of which the much-maligned apostle Paul writes in his letter to the Ephesians. For years I have watched with increasing dismay the destruction the feminist movement has wrought in the world, in the church, in Christian homes and marriages, and in personalities. I have studied the tortuous arguments of those who would persuade us that Galatians 3:28 cancels everything the author says elsewhere in his epistles about the vital distinctions between men and women. I have listened to

11

the endless discussions of Paul's rabbinical prejudice and cultural insularity. I have delved into treatises on the meaning of the Greek word *hypotassō* (ὑποτάσσω, "to arrange under," "to be under obedience," "to put under," "to subdue unto," "to subject to," "to be in subjection to," "to submit self unto"), and I have on a few occasions been asked (as a "traditionalist," whatever that means) to debate those who would rewrite history, literature, psychology, and the Bible itself to make them palatable to the woman of the late twentieth century. I have done practically everything but jump up and down and scream about it.

Here is a simple, sane, serious treatment of the subject by a man who loves God, respects women, and takes the inspiration of Scripture and the integrity of the apostles for granted. He deals with all the "difficult" texts. He tells us that his subject is not a clerical issue, nor is it hierarchical, situational, historical, or experimental; it is *biblical*. With that I agree wholeheartedly, but whether it can be settled, as he says, only by "scrupulous exegesis" I am not sure. I think it is even bigger, even deeper than that—a theological mystery representing Christ and the church, bigger than exegesis, deeper than our deepest understanding. And such things will never be "settled."

Read this book. The exegesis points to the mystery. Mysteries are things revealed, not explained. Mysteries are always unsettling.

ELISABETH ELLIOT
Magnolia, Massachusetts
August 1989

INTRODUCTION

Methodist, Baptist, and United Reformed churches have women ministers. Some Pentecostals have long had women pastors (Aimee Semple McPherson was one of the best known). The Church of England now ordains women to the diaconate, which is the last hurdle before full priesthood, and the Episcopal Church in the U.S.A. has ordained female priests and recently consecrated a female bishop. Quite suddenly a number of the new "house" churches (fellowships meeting in local homes) are appointing women elders.

Is this a biblical idea whose time has come, like the abolition of slavery? Or is it yet another case of Christians being conformed to the world? What is the Spirit saying to the churches?

Here is one side of the debate, probably best seen as "opposing the motion." The bulk of current publications is on the other side so the motion has already been effectively "proposed." The house has not yet divided; there is still an opportunity for all of us to reconsider the question and change our minds.

The chapters of this book first appeared as a series of articles in *Renewal* magazine by the invitation of its editor, Edward England; because I count him as a friend, he must not be held responsible for the contents!

The material was originally prepared for a European convention of "Women's Aglow" in West Germany. One lady said to me afterward: "We *heard* the truth from you, but we *saw* it in your wife." That remark will always be a beautiful compliment to the one who has been a better helpmate than I ever deserved; it could also be a damning indictment of me if my understanding of the Bible has been mistaken!

In making my views public, I realize I am swimming against a strong tide. I have faced the cost of doing this—in terms of lost opportunities of ministry (I *could* still be sound in other directions!), personal aspersions (it is easier to attack a messenger than a message) and, above all, impaired relationships (though real friends are those with whom one can agree to differ without loss of affection).

My deepest anxiety is that women readers will take it all personally, dismissing my exposition as an excuse for yet another chauvinist put-down. Recognizing what festering wounds there are from immoral exploitation and unjust suppression, I can only say that it is not in my heart to add to those hurts. To have done so unnecessarily would sit heavily on my conscience.

Why, then, raise the issue? Why pursue a viewpoint considered widely as both obsolete and offensive? There are two reasons why I have done this.

First, I happen to believe it is the truth. A skeptical

age that views truth as subjective and relative, reached by cultural consensus, finds it hard to conceive that sincere conviction *can* be based on the revealed mind of God rather than the concealed motives of man. I have already been accused of delighting in provocation, harboring a secret death wish in my ministry, compensating for social inadequacy and other variations of subconscious deviation. There may be some truth in any or all of these charges—but that is hardly an adequate criterion by which to judge these pages. Let the reader emulate the Bereans, who tested Paul's words by the touchstone of Scripture, hopefully with the same result (Acts 17:11)!

Second, departure from the truth carries serious danger, in both belief and behavior. I confess that when I began to study this controversy I did not realize how much was at stake. What looks like a simple difference over the *interpretation* of Scripture easily slips into a subtle debate about its *authority*. And behind it all, the very nature of the Godhead is being questioned. I became fully aware of this only after completing the articles—by reading Donald Bloesch's *The Battle for the Trinity* (Servant Publications, Ann Arbor, Michigan). When an evangelical theologian of his standing speaks of "an ominous drift toward goddess spirituality" and "a refurbished form of the old heresy of Gnosticism" in connection with this issue, we must at least take notice.

The perils are practical as well as theological. Discipline could be as much affected as doctrine. The problems of single and separated mothers in bringing up children, particularly boys, could spread to the churches. The link between dominant mothers and homosexual sons is already recognized.

We are obviously handling such far-reaching issues that in the *flesh* I would shrink from attempting it. However, I trust the *Holy Spirit* to lead us into all truth. If I have written what he approves, he will confirm this in the reader's spirit and give fruit for my labors. If not, I pray that this book will be quickly forgotten before it damages the body of Christ and that I will be forgiven my blindness!

Finally, this is not a treatise on marriage or the ministry of women (though there are implications for both); it is addressed solely to the question of *leadership* in the redeemed people of God, which I am thus far convinced must be male.

CHAPTER 1

AS IT WAS IN THE BEGINNING...

The church is trailing the world in opening the ranks of leadership to women, a bad situation from every angle. If the trend is right, the church ought to be *leading* the world. If it is wrong, the church ought not to be *following* the world.

The chapters in this book are based on the conviction that equality of status does not mean interchangeability of function. Since I am a charismatic evangelical (rather than an evangelical charismatic!), four assumptions are made before the debate begins.

First, *all* Scripture is inspired (2 Timothy 3:16 actually says "*ex*pired") by God and, rightly interpreted, has binding authority on Christians at all times and in all places.

Second, the Spirit *never* contradicts Scripture, since he would be contradicting himself.

Third, where Scripture is clear, no *further* revelation is needed from the Spirit.

Fourth, any part of Scripture must be understood in the context of the *whole* to be truly biblical. A text out of context is a pretext. The use of Galatians 3:28 and 1 Timothy 2:12 as proof-texts for feminism and sexism is a classic example of this abuse of Scripture, as we shall see.

Both Jesus and Paul appeal to the first two chapters of Genesis, particularly the second, when teaching on male/female relationships. God's original pattern becomes the guideline for redeemed behavior.

There are, as most readers recognize, two accounts of creation. Such duplication (as in Kings/Chronicles and the four Gospels) is the divine method of communicating different aspects of the whole truth. Distortion occurs when these are not held in proper tension, even as paradox. Feminism overemphasizes Genesis 1, and sexism does the same for chapter 2.

The first account of creation may be called *vertical.* Its viewpoint is up in the sky or even out in space. Looking *down* on planet earth from above, it is primarily concerned with the Creator ("God") as the originator of the earth and its inhabitants, particularly mankind (*adam,* a generic term covering male and female; see Genesis 5:2).

The second account we shall call the *horizontal.* Its viewpoint is down on the ground, looking *around.* The primary interest is in the relationships of "*the* man," now an individual (Adam), with his Creator (now "*Yahweh* God," with a specific as well as a generic name), with plants, animals and, finally, *the* woman.

In both accounts, one verse is in poetry (the language of the heart and its feelings), as distinct from prose (the language of the head and its thoughts). Significantly, both coincide with the introduction of sex! God composed the first love-song, and man the second.

Sexuality is common to both accounts and fundamental to both relationships: the vertical (between God and man), and the horizontal (between man and woman). There is a precise analogy between the two, on which the whole Bible rests. This is why the roles of men and women are never reversed, in either the Old or the New Testament.

Both chapters emphasize the difference between the sexes as well as their similarity, the variety as well as the unity. Contrast is essential to complementarity.

> To resemble himself God created mankind
> To reflect in themselves his own heart, will, and mind
> To relate to each other, male and female entwined
> *(with apologies to Moses)*

There is no need to discuss the meaning of "image" in Genesis 1:27. (Is it reflection or reproduction? Is it spiritual, intellectual, moral, emotional, or even physical?) The important fact for this debate is that *both* male and female bear the image. Men and women are the same species and radically different from all other species. They are thus equal in value, potential, and destiny. This is the first statement about gender in Scripture and is rightly seen as underlying all later revelation.

However, we must be careful not to read modern social controversy back into Scripture. Although equality of status may be a legitimate deduction from this verse, it is doubtful if this message was the main intention of the author (human or divine). Taken at face value, the verse emphasizes the similarity of human beings (male and female) to their Creator and their difference from all other creatures.

Why should sexuality be mentioned in the same breath as the divine image? Is there a connection?

Some would deny any link, taking "image" as a purely spiritual attribute and "male and female" as primarily physical, that part of man more like the animals than God. But "male and female" is never used of fish, animals, or birds—only of man! And it occurs in this *poetic* verse, not in the prose command to multiply, which follows. Sexuality has spiritual significance.

Others postulate a "split image," in which only man and woman *together* can be the whole representation of God (men showing his justice, women his mercy, etc.). If this were so, Jesus could hardly be the "exact representation" of God (Hebrews 1:3) or have the fullness of God dwelling in him (Colossians 1:19).

A third approach emphasizes "corporate personality." God is tripersonal, plural ("Let *us* make man in *our* image" [Genesis 1:26, emphasis added]). Man and woman *together* reflect Father, Son, and Spirit. If this thinking is valid, there would be subordination as well as equality in "manhood," as in the Godhead. But the Bible never draws the parallel. One would have to speculate as to why Jesus never married or even why there are not three sexes!

The simplest explanation is probably the best. The verse is emphasizing no more and no less than that *both* sexes bear the same divine image. Whenever this basic truth is overlooked, humans will exploit, abuse, and slander one another.

But equality does not mean interchangeability. A cylinder head and a crankcase may be of the same material, size, weight, and cost—but they cannot be exchanged!

Some have seen grounds for identity of function in Genesis 1:28, where God tells male and female to rule and subdue the earth. But he is telling them *both* to do it together, not *either* of them to do it separately. Within the shared task, their particular roles may be quite different, as is certainly the case with the command to "increase in number" and "fill the earth," in the same verse.

If Genesis 1 highlights those features common to the sexes, Genesis 2 emphasizes those not shared. And God created woman . . . from a different material, for a different purpose, and at a different time. These three dissimilarities are all mentioned in the New Testament as significant for the roles of men and women.

Woman was made *from* man, not dust. This might be thought to indicate the incompleteness of the man (and the "reason" he seeks union with a wife rather than parents; see Genesis 2:24); but Paul uses this to support the *headship* of the man (1 Corinthians 11:8), possibly recalling that she came from his "side."

Woman was made *for* man; the reverse is not true (1 Corinthians 11:9). Her primary function is in relation to him; his was already established without reference to her (Genesis 2:15). The word *help* in no way implies inferiority, since it is often used of God's assistance. Neither does it imply identity, since God's help is in terms of support, sympathy, and strength rather than substituting for man in his task.

Woman was made *after* man. His priority in time has other implications. The firstborn carries responsibility for and authority over later arrivals, as Paul indicates in 1 Timothy 2:13.

Any one of these three aspects of woman's creation would not conclusively establish her subordination to man, but the cumulative effect of all three points in this direction, especially in the light of their application in the "apostles' doctrine." That Adam himself understood them in this way is indicated by his calling her "woman."

Naming in Scripture is an expression of authority. God names "man" (Genesis 5:2) and the stars (Isaiah 40:26; astronomy began when man did!). "Man" named the animals when God "brought" them to him; and he named the "woman" when God "brought" her to him. He is not rebuked for taking this authority. Nor is it valid to object that "woman" is not a name since it is generic rather than specific (as is claimed by those who see such authority as the result of the fall, when Adam called her "Eve"); the names that Adam "called" the animals (Genesis 2:19) were also of this category (rhinoceros rather than Rodney!). Incidentally, a legacy of his action is to be found in a wife taking her husband's surname after marriage.

Genesis 1 and 2, then, present us with truth in the form of paradox. Men and women are the same, only different. They are both like God, but unlike each other. They are equal, yet unequal.

Such paradoxes in Scripture (the paradox of predestination and free will is the most obvious) can be experienced in life, but not explained in logic. Rationalized systems of doctrine can do justice to only one side of the coin (hence Calvin*ism* and Arminian*ism;* in this debate, sex*ism* and femin*ism*). Nor is there a balance to be found midway between the two poles. Only by emphasizing *both* apparent opposites can the whole truth be preached and practiced.

The paradox of gender is fundamental to the whole Bible, where the male/female relationship is seen as the best analogy for the divine/human relationship. *Both* relationships are characterized by equal and unequal factors. God and man can relate face-to-face because they bear the same image, yet man is subordinate to God. The same dual aspect applies to men and women.

The analogy is specifically sexual. The male represents the divine side of the partnership; the female represents the human. Both Jews and Christians have seen this analogy in the Song of Solomon (which never mentions God, like that other romance, Esther). As well as affirming sensual love (its primary message), the book may be validly expounded as an analogy for spiritual love. This is quite different from treating it as an allegory, finding esoteric meanings in erotic details. (The "two breasts" are the Old and New Testaments! Presumably "between breasts" refers to the Apocrypha!)

The analogy recurs many times in Scripture. See, for example, Ezekiel 16, where Jerusalem is variously described as an abandoned baby girl, developing in puberty, courted and married, enthroned as queen, and finally turning to prostitution. The New Testament follows the Old. Jesus uses the feminine word for his church (Matthew 16:18); he loves *her* and gives himself for *her* (Ephesians 5:25; note that here the analogy is inverted: the divine/human relationship becomes the pattern for husband/wife relationships).

The fundamental feature in the analogy is the correspondence between the male and the divine, the female and the human. The parallel is nonreversible. Husband and wife are no more interchangeable than God and man!

God reveals himself in *male* terms. He *is* our father, not our mother; our king, not our queen; our husband, not our wife (Baal, not Astarte). God incarnate had to be a *man*. An androgynous Christ, much less an effeminate one, would be a distorted image (Holman Hunt's painting, *The Light of the World*, is unfortunate, the hair, face, and figure taken from female models).

Christian feminists constantly refer to some statements in the Bible applying feminine terminology to both God and Jesus, implying that in some mysterious way they are bisexual and would be thought of more accurately as such. The most frequently quoted texts are Deuteronomy 32:18; Isaiah 42:14; 49:15; Matthew 23:27; and Luke 15:8.

The first thing to say about these is that they are of the nature of simile rather than definition. God, in some respects, is *like* a mother (actually, Isaiah 49:15 contrasts him to a mother; God is *unlike* the best mother!); but this does not mean he *is* a mother. Second, the proportion of these feminine references is infinitesimal, compared to the male. What really neutralizes any attempt to find theological significance in these statements is the fact that the same tiny percentage of feminine metaphors is applied to Moses (Numbers 11:12), the twelve apostles (John 16:21–22), and Paul (Galatians 4:19; 1 Thessalonians 2:7). No one in his right mind would take this to mean they were bisexual!

Men can "give birth" to a project, by cooperating with "bosom" friends, "nursing" it in its infant stages, finally "aborting" the mission, because it does not work out as originally "conceived"—and all this without their sexual orientation being called into question! To claim, as one recent writer, that "deity was *as much* able to be spoken of in female as in male symbols" is not even statistically accurate.

C. S. Lewis was nearer the biblical mark when he pointed out,

> Goddesses have, of course, been worshipped: many religions have had priestesses. But they are religions quite different from Christianity . . . a child who had been taught to pray to a mother in heaven would have a religious life radically different from that of a Christian child. *(God in the Dock)*

This comment indicates just how much is at stake. We are in danger of changing the image of God into a reflection of the sexual confusion of our secular society, a deity who has more in common with Hermaphroditus (the son of Hermes and Aphrodite in Greek mythology, who became joined in one body with the nymph Salmacis) than with Yahweh, the Father of Jesus. The biblical word for this is *idolatry*.

CHAPTER 2

A PATRIARCHAL
PEOPLE

The Garden of Eden has disappeared and, with it, the original order of creation. The fall from innocence distorted all relationships, particularly between men and women, destroying primeval harmony (*shalom*).

Genesis 3 is here taken as fact rather than fiction, history rather than myth, one man's epoch-making choice rather than Everyman's existential choices. A talking lizard (not a snake; it had legs) is no greater problem than Balaam's ass; fruit with spiritual efficacy no more than the Lord's Supper.

We consider only two aspects: its inference for the gender question and its interpretation in the New Testament. We separate the two stages: the crime and its punishment.

Chronologically, Eve was the first to sin. That is because Satan approached her first. Why did he do so? "Divide to conquer" is an ancient military maxim; one is easier to tackle than two. But why Eve rather than Adam? Was this a deliberate defiance of God's order, tempting Eve to take the lead, to adopt the masculine role? Or was Eve more vulnerable in some way (which might imply Satan's cowardice!)? Note that Satan is *masculine* (no feminist has ever claimed otherwise!) and is portrayed as a mental seducer, being the "more crafty."

The New Testament enlarges on this point: Adam was not deceived, whereas Eve was (1 Timothy 2:14). This *might* mean that Eve was less culpable (she thought she was doing right, whereas Adam *knew* he was doing wrong), but it more probably means that Eve was more vulnerable to being seduced in mind. The context is Paul's practice of prohibiting instruction by women; however uncomfortable we may feel with his line of thought, he seems to be saying that Eve, as typical woman, was more liable to be misled and therefore more likely to mislead.

Eve acknowledged her "deception," even used it as an excuse (Genesis 3:13). Made in God's own likeness, she was fooled into a desire to be like God. She recognized the *distortion* of God's word ("*any* tree") but failed to spot an outright *denial* of it ("you will not surely die"). Nor did she discern the underlying appeal to moral autonomy and unilateral independence. She took immediate action based on her own judgment, not even consulting her husband, much less her Maker.

That Adam followed her with neither argument nor protest put him in the feminine role, which may explain why, *theologically*, Adam was the first to sin.

The New Testament holds him responsible for introducing sin and death to the human race (Romans 5:12) rather than Eve (a judgment not always reflected in church attitudes). This is not based on any supposed innocence in Eve because she "thought it was all right" (God punished her as well, and her action made her "a sinner," in spite of her deception; see 1 Timothy 2:14). It does mean that Adam is regarded as basically responsible for the whole situation, for her as well as for himself. He could have and should have rebuked her and interceded for her. Instead, he tried to shift blame to her (Genesis 3:12), not realizing that "she led me" implies "I followed her." In taking a feminine role, Adam was abdicating his position.

The punishment fitted the criminals rather than the crime. But was the sentence a penalty or a consequence, a personal addition to their circumstances or an impersonal, inevitable, inherent outcome of their action? Our answer relates to our interpretation of the wrath of God and hell itself. Space forbids debate. The writer takes the view that the penalties were as personal and additional as being expelled from Eden. However, the practical results are the same, whichever view is taken.

The Fall introduced *struggle* into their respective spheres of activity (this became the watchword of men like Darwin, Marx, Nietzsche, and Hitler). Where there had been harmony, now there would be hostility. Order gives way to opposition, accord to alienation.

Note that their separate spheres of activity as man and woman are *already* differentiated—Adam will be affected in his daily work, Eve in her family relationships. The Fall did not introduce this differentiation; it merely damaged it (cf. Genesis 2:15, 18).

Adam is addressed *first*, since he carries prime responsibility in the partnership. Banished from the orchard to the field, he will survive only with great effort against opposing factors (thorns and thistles are far more formidable in the Middle East than in Europe). No mention is made of his marital relations, nor is *he* told to "rule" his wife.

Eve is also punished, but in relation to her family. In "childbearing" (birth process rather than upbringing) her pain (physical rather than mental, and *not* menstrual) is to be increased (not introduced). In relation to her husband, her "desire will be *to*" him, an unusual Hebraism that means an ambition to control, manipulate, and possess someone (as its occurrence in Genesis 4:7 clearly shows). That is, having led her husband into sin, she must now live with a continuing urge to subordinate him to her wish and will.

His reaction will be not only to resist this takeover, but to use his greater strength to rule her. Male domination is the inevitable result of this struggle for supremacy of wills. In Genesis 3:16 lies the real explanation for the centuries of exploitation and suppression of women, against which feminism is validly protesting. Incidentally, it also means that a husband who is henpecked has *chosen* to capitulate, usually for the sake of domestic peace.

The advent of *rule* to describe marriage (a word hitherto used only for *other* creatures and of *both* man and woman; see Genesis 1:28) was not the introduction of subordination but the exaggeration of it (in much the same way as pain in childbearing was increased). Responsibility for direction in the male became reaction into domination. The male-directed Garden is now a male-dominated jungle. Each sex sees the other as an object (rather than a subject) to serve its own purposes.

This situation can be remedied only by divine grace, by redemption rather than legislation or revolution. God's strategy is to plant on earth a community of men and women who will live as Adam and Eve did, in his creation order (except for their nudity, which will never recur, even in heaven). The first such people was the nation of Israel, to which we now turn. Were the social roles of men and women equal and interchangeable among them? Or hierarchical? To answer this, we look at four periods, each with a different category of leadership.

1. **Patriarchs** (Abraham to Joseph)

The very word (a biblical one) gives the answer for this initial phase. God is the "God of Abraham, Isaac and Jacob"; he does not link himself with the names of Sarah, Rebekah, and Rachel. Life was very patriarchal.

Inheritance passes through the sons (the twelve sons of Jacob becoming the twelve tribes of Israel), not the daughters (there is no tribe of Dinah).

The patriarchs' wives were attractive to look at because they were attractive to live with, because they happily accepted a subordinate position relative to their husbands ("lord and master"!)—all of which information comes not from Genesis, but from a *married* apostle in the New Testament who uses these marital attitudes as a model for Christian wives (1 Peter 3:1–6), who are likewise exhorted to "submit." "Meek and gentle" may not summarize contemporary ideals of womanhood, but that does not invalidate their relevance to redeemed humanity.

In passing, we mention Joseph's "manly" resistance to Potiphar's wife, an example unheeded by Samson, Ahab, and even David and Solomon.

2. Prophets (Moses to Samuel)

There were prophets before Moses (Genesis 20:7; Psalm 105:15; Jude 14) and many after Samuel (Elijah, Elisha, Isaiah, Jeremiah, Ezekiel, etc.), but it was during this period that they held the reins of national leadership. Significantly, it was *only* at this time that a woman came into such national prominence (see comments below).

The divine laws given at Sinai to guide their communal life represent a major shift in the evaluation of women, when judged by contemporary pagan legislation (for example, the Code of Hammurabi or the laws of Egypt). It is unfair to highlight remaining inequalities (injustices?) in the Mosaic legislation until this giant leap for mankind (treating women as persons rather than possessions) has been acknowledged. And we need to remember the laws were framed by God rather than Moses. Any shortfall from the "ideal" of creation was of his making, presumably because restoration could not be total until the full grace of salvation was available.

There are, therefore, *traces* of a "double standard," with more male than female "rights" (for example, in the matter of divorce). Polygamy is accepted, though not approved. Female slaves and prisoners may be treated as property. However, as we shall see, these inequalities are not taken up into the new covenant.

Moses delegated his authority to seventy elders, all men, thus continuing the patriarchal structure. However, prophecy was a ministry of both men and women (Aaron's sister, Miriam, is a specific example). Already there seems to be a distinction between the human authority inherent in an "office" of leadership and the divine authority of a revelation, whoever communicates it. Passing on a message from God (as he has given it, without expansion, explanation, or application) is not seen as exercising leadership authority.

When Moses "numbered" Israel, only the men over twenty, able to serve in the army, were counted (Numbers 1:3; and even among them, those in their first year of marriage were excluded from service). The census totaled about six hundred thousand, instead of over two million, had women and children been included. It was never considered the responsibility of women to defend themselves or their families, in contrast to the modern Israeli army.

This has a bearing on the case of Deborah (the "busy bee"). Judges were raised up to deal with national defense (Judges 2:16), but they had a moral as well as a military function, namely, to preserve internal holiness that prevented external attack (Judges 2:17–19). The latter role was more prophetic than judicial. Their qualification was charismatic, and they were not agents of centralized government (Gideon refused to found a royal dynasty, on the ground of divine rule; see Judges 8:22–23).

However, in between averting external dangers, some judges settled internal disputes, among them Deborah who thus "judged" (NIV "led" is not helpful) Israel. Three facts about her are stated: she was a "wife" (of "Flash" Lappidoth), a "prophetess" (passing on divine words), and she settled "disputes." The impression is left of a Hebrew equivalent of the Delphic oracle; she was able to bring an inspired word of wisdom or knowledge to bear on each case.

Unlike other judges, she did *not* lead when invasion threatened but delegated (or, more accurately, the Lord delegated through her) this task to the man, Barak. He, with less than masculine courage or chivalry, insisted on taking her into battle, ensuring his forfeiture of the honor of victory (Judges 4:6–9).

Her triumphal song praised the Lord that the "princes" (i.e., ruling men) took "the lead," showing that her attitude was maternal (a mother in Israel) rather than matriarchal. She was no Boadicea or Joan of Arc, in spite of the apparent shortage of strong men.

3. Kings (Saul to Zedekiah)

The most obvious feature in this period is the absence of queens, which other nations had (Egypt, Sheba and later, Ethiopia).

Mosaic law had provision for kings, though in God's permissive rather than purposive will (Deuteronomy 17:14–20; 1 Samuel 8). To ensure a succession of kings, God would have to ensure the birth of *sons* (1 Kings 2:4).

Though there were no queens, there continued to be prophetesses, of whom Huldah is a representative. She influenced the king, as did other women, for better and worse (Jezebel and Athaliah, the "queen mother").

From King Lemuel came the glowing account of the "perfect" wife (the description is too vivid not to refer to an actual person); the last chapter in Proverbs is in stark contrast to earlier warnings in that book about women to avoid! It is important to note that she engaged in many activities outside the home—and in making money as well as showing mercy (though today's leisured wives might observe that she did not seize the opportunity to surpass her husband in spiritual knowledge by attending religious meetings without him!).

4. Priests (Zerubbabel to Caiaphas)

Though after the exile there were prophets (Ezekiel to Malachi) and some "kings" (Maccabean, Hasmonean), the continuity of national leadership now lay with the high priests. Of necessity, by divine law, all were male.

When the prophetic word ceased, study concentrated on the written word of the Lord. Inevitably, legalism increased, bringing harsh rather than humanitarian attitudes. The familiar division between the liberal and the conservative (Sadducee and Pharisee, Hillel and Shammai) interpretation of Scripture led to differences in doctrine and ethics.

But the debate was exclusively *male*. Women were not even taught by the rabbis. They were segregated in worship, both in the synagogue and in the temple (the court of the women), though there is no record of them having to veil their heads. Men thanked God they were not born a Gentile, a slave, or . . . a woman (a prayer from tradition, not Scripture)!

Since the one major spiritual ministry of women (prophecy) was now closed (God remained silent for four centuries), the whole religious scene became exclusively male. However, the predictions of earlier prophets, two in particular, were treasured by simple folk (the "poor").

One, that there would someday be another *prophet* like Moses to lead the people into full freedom (Deuteronomy 18:15). This expectation was coalescing with the hope of another Davidic *king*.

Two, that the Spirit would be poured out on the whole people of God (Joel 2:28). The prophetic ministry would be restored on an unparalleled scale: *all* men and women and not just *some* men and women (as formerly).

The stage was set for the coming of the King (and, therefore, the kingdom). What changes would he make? In particular, would he abolish the patriarchal pattern of leadership that had prevailed for so many centuries? Would the outpouring of the Spirit on all *women* significantly alter their place in the redeemed community?

CHAPTER 3

BEHOLD THE MAN

Few, if any, deny that Old Testament society was patriarchal. To be ruled by women was a symptom of moral and spiritual decadence (Isaiah 3:12). Normal leadership was male.

But we live in the new covenant, free (in theory at least!) from Sabbath, tithe, and kosher diet. The laws of Moses are "obsolete" (Hebrews 8:13), replaced by "Christ's law," which is "the perfect law that gives freedom" (1 Corinthians 9:21; James 1:25). Does this freedom include the total emancipation of women? Has Jesus abolished sex distinction and discrimination?

Jesus said absolutely nothing on the subject, which is an astonishing omission in view of his many criticisms of other aspects of Jewish tradition. Apart from granting equal nonrights of divorce and remarriage to husbands *and* wives (Mark 10:11f.), he made no specific reference to feminine "rights."

His views can only be inferred from his attitudes and actions. When such a procedure is used to establish dogma, it is peculiarly vulnerable to subjective prejudice. The emphasis must be on the facts rather than our interpretation of them.

Fact: Jesus was a *man*. Not bisexual, not homosexual. We saw earlier that the "exact representation of God" and the fullness of God could not have dwelt in a woman. A divinity revealed in male terms could be incarnate only in masculine form.

Fact: Jesus was a *bachelor*. Other founders of world religions have married (from Muhammad to Gandhi), but he was complete and sufficient in himself. His "bride" and "wedding supper" (Revelation 19:9; 22:17) are the results of our need, not his.

Fact: Jesus' relationships with women were unique in the annals of religious history and in stark contrast to the Jewish rabbis of his day. Over forty references to women in the Gospels demand attention and analysis. Actions can speak louder than words.

Fact: Jesus ministered *to* women. This is clearest in Luke's gospel, but a feature of all four Gospels.

He included them in his *public* teaching, drawing illustrations from the experience of men and women— the seed and the yeast (Matthew 13:31–33), the lost sheep and the lost coin (Luke 15:4–10), the importunate householder and the persistent widow (Luke 11:5–8; 18:2–5). Is it coincidence that the male parable always comes *first*?

He gave them *private* instruction. Mary in the home at Bethany and the woman at the well in Samaria could represent many other such conversations.

He performed *miracles* for women, from Peter's mother-in-law to the widow of Nain. Particular feminine diseases of menstrual or dorsal nature received his compassionate relief. Mary Magdalene was not alone in experiencing his "deliverance" ministry.

All this was contrary to Jewish tradition and convention. If the story of the woman caught in adultery is authentic (John 7:53–8:11 is not in some manuscripts), he even sat lightly to Mosaic legislation (which, incidentally, demanded the stoning of the man caught in adultery as well), averting her punishment.

No one treated women with more respect, even those whom others despised ("Simon, do you *see* this woman, as she really is?" [Luke 7:44, author's paraphrase]). He understood them; they understood him (Matthew 27:19).

Fact: Jesus received ministry *from* women. This began before his birth (notice the women in his genealogy: Matthew 1:3, 5–6, 16). Since he was the only person who ever chose to be born, *he* decided to be suckled at Mary's breast and have his swaddling cloths changed by her. However, note that his foster father, Joseph, was still given the delegated authority to name the baby (Matthew 1:21). And we need to understand his increasing disassociation from his mother after his public ministry began, which reached its climax at the cross. After one fleeting mention of Mary just before Pentecost (when she presumably spoke in tongues with the rest), her ministry is apparently "finished." Her unique contribution to the world's redemption has been grotesquely overestimated by Catholics and grossly underestimated by Protestants. Charismatic understanding is reaching a truer estimate of her role.

Jesus was not above accepting help from women. He asked the Samaritan woman for a drink (though he never got it; she was too fascinated with his views!). Women traveled with him and his disciples (Mark 15:41; Luke 8:4), though Scripture hints their ministry was of a practical nature (purchasing food and clothes, cooking, and washing?); and there were "many" who did this, some of them married (what did their husbands think?).

What is there *still* to be said about Martha and Mary? Perhaps that Martha's cooking was normally welcome to Jesus, but on one occasion he needed fellowship rather than food, so Mary had prepared "the better dish" (i.e., for him rather than for herself). Was it on this occasion he told her about his death and the lack of opportunity it would give for a proper embalming? Certainly she did something about this on his next visit.

It is a cliché that women were last at the cross and first at the tomb. To get the whole truth, we need to realize they ran far less risk to themselves than male followers of an accused insurrectionist (a risk that John did take; see John 19:26). And it was the women's task to anoint corpses. However, Jesus himself did choose to appear *first* to a woman and to trust her to communicate the incredible news to the men. By contrast *their* cowardice and unbelief are honestly reported in Scripture (though the women had *seen*, whereas the men had only *heard;* they also believed when they saw, Thomas being no more skeptical than the other ten). That women are often more ready to trust than men is both a strength and a weakness.

So far we have discerned no apparent discrimination between the sexes in Jesus' ministry. But we have not yet told the whole story. In particular, we have not discussed his attitude to women *in leadership*. Again, with one outstanding exception, we can only deduce this indirectly.

For example, the Gospels record his negative reactions to women who tell him what to do. It happens first at Cana, when his mother hints that a miracle would be in order. His rebuke is a Hebrew colloquialism for "Don't interfere"; and his addressing her as "Woman" could be either a reminder of her gender or, more likely, a repudiation of her maternal authority, to which he had hitherto been subject.

In Sidon, the Syro-Phoenician woman comes in for rather brusque treatment when she invades the privacy of Jesus' "vacation" (Mark 7:24–30). His rebuke is in sharp contrast to the similar approach of a Gentile *man* (Matthew 8:10), though other factors could explain the difference. And she did not accept it as a put-down!

Martha's sharp tongue "orders" Jesus—and she receives a cut from *his* two-edged sword (John 11:40–41)! But she was the first woman, as Peter had been the first man, to recognize and verbalize who Jesus actually was (compare Matthew 16:16 with John 11:27).

However, these encounters may not be relevant to the issue of leadership in general. There were times when Jesus dealt similarly with men who sought his assistance (Luke 12:14).

More significant were the occasions when Jesus was accompanied only by some of his *male* followers, by his specific choice. The most surprising was the raising of Jairus's daughter, when the usual understanding of a domestic tragedy would make feminine presence desirable.

The Transfiguration is more puzzling because of its major significance. Why was this profound perspective on his person and purpose shared only with men (and then only three of them)?

The Last Supper, the final "Jewish" and the first "Christian" Passover meal, was limited to men only, even though women had followed Jesus into Jerusalem. The "secret sign" of the arrangements was to be a *man* carrying a pitcher of water! The new covenant was inaugurated in a totally male context; since it was private rather than public, one can only speculate about the reasons. (Did Jesus not trust women to keep the secret? Was he protecting them from possible arrest?) The only thing that is clear is that *both* men and women partook of this meal on subsequent occasions, so the all-male original was not seen as a precedent for the young church.

Only men were present in Gethsemane, and Luke's language actually implies that only men witnessed the Ascension (Acts 1:11).

Again, all this may not be significant for the question of church leadership, but it needs to be noted that on some occasions Jesus deliberately chose to be accompanied by three or twelve men, without any women.

Still more significant is the use of the word *disciple*. It is never specifically used of women, even of those who followed him. Discipleship is spelled out in male terms: "If anyone comes to me and does not hate . . . his wife" (Luke 14:26; no mention of "her husband"). This may be due to the fact that following Jesus in the days of his *flesh* could only be itinerant (John 6:66); the Lord might call a husband to leave his domestic commitment, but it is highly unlikely he would tell a wife to do so.

The seventy apostles sent out in Luke 10:1–24 are addressed as men (Today's English Version) when the teams of two return. There is no trace of Jesus' calling women to follow him, though he allowed them to do so (Matthew 27:55; Mark 15:41; Luke 23:49); nor did he ever send them out on missions. There are echoes of this usage of *disciple* for men only elsewhere in the New Testament (Acts 21:5 speaks of "all the disciples and their wives and children"). But again, we must be careful not to read too much into this.

The one indisputable fact is that Jesus chose twelve *men* to be his apostles. No specific reason is given. Yet because this was the nearest he came during his lifetime to giving a leadership structure to his church, we must explore the implications. Five major interpretations are current; let's look at them in ascending order of likelihood.

First, a *synagogue* cannot be established until it has ten men; Jesus was called "Rabbi" because he had this quorum. *But* we do not know if this rule was applied then and Jesus was building his church rather than starting a synagogue (the word means, literally, "come together").

Second, the apostles were to be *witnesses* to the Resurrection, and no woman was acceptable as a legal witness in Jewish courts. *But* he was not looking for legal witnesses; rather, he was sending men and women into the world to "gossip" the good news (as one translation of Acts 8:4 puts it).

Third, this was one major concession to contemporary *culture* that Jesus made; female apostles would have been just too much for those days. *But* when did Jesus ever display such diplomacy, which was totally out of character? Even his enemies admitted he put truth before convention (Matthew 22:16). He had done enough other things to violate custom for this one to be such an exception! And it would have been an ideal opportunity to establish the "new humanity," by choosing six men and six women (it would also have saved the time and trouble we are spending on this debate!).

Fourth, it can be seen as a *symbolic* gesture, an acted parable, and no more. In choosing twelve men, he was inviting people to see a parallel with the twelve sons of Jacob and draw the conclusion that he was founding a "new Israel" (though the name *Israel*, used over seventy times in the New Testament, is always applied to the Jewish nation rather than the church, with one doubtful exception in Galatians 6:16). *But* if his act was *only* symbolic, it is difficult to see why he himself and later teachers put such emphasis on the Twelve (e.g., 1 Corinthians 15:5). He promised they would exercise a judicial function in the future (Matthew 19:28) and their names would be on the foundations of the New Jerusalem. Indeed, had he chosen six men and six women, the symbolism of a new Israel would have remained intact and underlined the "new" constitution more effectively.

Fifth, we are left with the most natural meaning: namely, the *patriarchal* nature of government among the people of God continues from the old into the new covenant. Jesus would not put women in a position of directing men. However offensive this may be in our day, it is the interpretation most consistent with the Scriptures (Old Testament) in which Jesus believed and those writings of the apostles later recognized as Scripture.

From among these men, Peter was chosen to be the first pastor, and he became the first preacher after Pentecost. The foundation of the church was male.

Jesus announced no basic change in the roles of men and women. Of course, his silence on the subject could be due to the fact that there were many things he could not *then* tell them (John 16:12) but would later communicate through his Spirit of truth. Certainly he said a great deal through the apostles after Pentecost. In the next chapter we shall consider both the practice of the apostles (in Acts) and their preaching on the issue (in the Epistles).

The paradox of Genesis 1 and 2 remains. Men and women are equal, yet unequal; the same, yet different. Jesus' own attitudes and actions are totally consistent with his Father's original creation.

CHAPTER 4

COME BACK, PETER

Jesus' attitudes toward and relationships with women provide an impeccable model for social and spiritual dealings between the sexes; but they provide scant guidance for leadership or ministry in the church. Apart from two isolated but significant references to the "church" (universal in Matthew 16:18 and local in Matthew 18:17) and his choice of twelve *men* to be her foundation, he gave no direct teaching on ecclesiastical structure. Nor did he announce any radical departure from the patriarchal government of God's holy people characteristic of Israel.

However, the four Gospels cannot be made either a final or the complete basis for Christian doctrine. Preceding the complete salvation history of the Cross, Resurrection, Ascension, and Pentecost, the Gospels are transitional in many aspects of Christian teaching. For example, the dying thief cannot be taken as a paradigm of Christian initiation, in view of the post-Easter meaning of water baptism and the post-Pentecost experience of Spirit baptism, to say nothing of the fuller content of faith in the Lord Jesus after these events.

To put it another way, the church is to be *apostolic*, as well as one, holy, and catholic. Her belief and behavior are not simply attempts to put the Gospels into practice; they rest squarely on the deeds of the apostles (in Acts) and their word (in the Epistles). Orthodoxy and orthopraxy are the results of "continuing steadfastly in the apostles' doctrine," to which we now turn.

Since the book of Acts follows the Gospels and precedes the Epistles, it is appropriate to begin here. Acts is not all descriptive narrative (see chapters 7 and 15), any more than the Epistles are all didactic discourse (see Galatians 1 and 2). They illuminate each other (a good example of a self-explanatory Bible). Narrative can contribute to doctrine (1 Corinthians 10:6, 11; 2 Timothy 3:16). Whether we regard Luke's second volume of memoirs as the "acts" of the apostles, the "acts" of the Holy Spirit (he is mentioned at least forty times in the first thirteen chapters), or the continued "acts" of Jesus himself (1:1), we have here a picture of the church as it really was, as it was meant to be throughout church history, and as it could be today by the power of the Spirit of Jesus.

As in "volume one," women are frequently mentioned (1:14; 2:18; 5:14; 6:1; 8:3, 12; 9:39–41; 16:13–15; 17:4, 12, 34; 18:2, 26; 21:5, 9; 22:4; 25:13; 26:30). In chapter 1 they are praying with the men, and in chapter 2 they are "prophesying" with the men (Paul encourages both activities by women in 1 Corinthians 11:5).

The coming of the Spirit at Pentecost (which was also

the coming of the kingdom with power; see Mark 9:1) established the prophethood of all believers. Peter calls it "prophecy" either because unintelligible speech was akin to early prophetic expression (as in 1 Samuel 10:5–11) or, more likely, because the "languages" were intelligible to the hearers (Acts 2:11). In any case, the manifestation of tongues was not totally new to Jews, though it was more usually a sign of judgment (Genesis 11:7; Isaiah 28:11; 1 Corinthians 14:21–22). Nor was it a new thing that *women* were prophesying. What was new was that *all* flesh was doing it, regardless of age, sex, and class. It was a change in degree, not kind. There had been prophetesses before Pentecost (Luke 2:36), as there would be afterward (Acts 21:9).

The term *disciple* is occasionally used exclusively of males (Acts 21:5; and possibly 19:1–7), but is clearly now used of women (9:36)—and of *resident* rather than itinerant followers of the Way. Men and women together "suffer" discipline inside the church (5:1–11) and persecution outside (8:3; 9:2).

Women play a key role in the planting of new colonies of the kingdom—at Philippi (16:14), Thessalonica (17:4), Berea (17:12), and Athens (17:34), for example.

Priscilla and Aquila (her name coming before her husband's probably indicates a high social origin) work together in enlightening Apollos (Acts 18:24–26). In assessing the significance of this occasion, we need to note that the verb *teach* is not used on this occasion. They did it together, and it was a private context in their home, not a public one in church.

All this is very much in line with the pattern already

observed in the Gospels, where water baptism was practiced on both men and women (unlike circumcision, which was given only to sons as heirs), and Spirit baptism was promised to both men and women.

But as in the Gospels, there is another side to the picture: Only *men* were present at the Ascension (or, at least, only men were addressed by the angels; see Acts 1:11). Judas had to be replaced in his ministry (the *only* person to be described as *episcopos, apostolos,* and *diakonos;* 1:17, 20, 25) by a *man* (1:21), even though women were the first witnesses of the Resurrection.

At Pentecost, though men and women "prophesied," only a *man* preached, while eleven *men* "stood" with him. (The fact that the rest remained sitting indicates it was not in the Upper Room, but in the temple porch at the hour of prayer: the crowd *came* to them.) In fact, *there is no record of any woman preaching or teaching in the book of Acts.* By itself, this could lead to a precarious argument from silence; however, the Epistles may confirm that it is not an accidental omission.

Surprisingly, when a need arose in the catering department, seven *men* were chosen so that the apostles would not have to spend time serving tables! A church today would be most likely to appoint a committee of ladies, as better suited both to understanding widows and to distributing food. (However, the author recalls that the ladies of the Millmead Centre in Guildford, where he was a pastor, nominated a man as catering deacon, though the revised constitution made full provision for "deaconesses"!)

Why a group of *men* to cater for *widows?* Because of

the need to settle a dispute (hence the qualification: "full of wisdom")? Because the job involved supervision as well as service (*episcopos* as well as *diakonos*, therefore "full of the Spirit")? Or because they were widows, with no man to defend their rights? The last explanation is most probable (Psalm 68:5).

Early missionary (apostolic) teams were made up of a minimum of two men (as in Luke 10:1)—Paul and Barnabas, Paul and Mark, Paul and Silas (always Paul!). There is no mention of women traveling with them, though this may be inferred from the Epistles (Romans 16:3; 1 Corinthians 9:5; Philippians 4:3) and would be consistent with Jesus himself.

The doctrinal dispute over circumcision was settled by men. Acts 15 describes not an ecumenical council, but a gathering of one church (Jerusalem), whose orthodoxy had been challenged by another (Antioch). After an open declaration of the charge, a smaller group of men withdrew to discuss the issue—the "apostles" whose concern would be the universal *doctrine* and the "elders" whose duty would be the local *discipline* of teachers based in the city. The result was announced by a man (James) and communicated more widely by two men (Judas and Silas), who were "prophets" (Acts 15:32).

In all this, there is a striking resemblance to Old Testament history, at least on the human side of the story. The proportion of attention given to men and women respectively is much the same in the books of Judges and Acts, for example. In both books men play the major role (Gideon, Abimelech, Jephthah, Samson, etc., in the one; Peter, John, James, Paul, etc., in the other). It could even be argued that Deborah had greater responsibility in her day than Tabitha, Lydia, and Priscilla in theirs! Some Christian feminist writers have been as critical of Luke's writings as of Paul's, accusing him of a patronizing attitude, in spite of his more frequent references to women. What can be said is that the book of Acts reveals no radical change in gender roles subsequent to Pentecost. Leadership is still male.

It therefore comes as no surprise to find that the apostolic teaching in the epistles contains a similar consistency with the Scriptures of the Old Testament.

James in his letter says nothing about the roles of men and women, but his definition of pure religion as looking after widows and orphans (James 1:27) is straight from the Old Testament (Isaiah 1:17). The apparent indifference to the loneliness (and, often, helplessness!) of *widowers*, in both Testaments, is due to the basic problem of widows and orphans—namely, not having a *man* to protect and provide for them.

Peter has much more explicit teaching on our subject. It is amazing that Paul has drawn so much feminist fire when Peter goes just as far, if not further, in teaching a subordinate role for wives. And Peter spoke as a married man (Mark 1:30; 1 Corinthians 9:5), whereas we do not know for sure whether Paul was a bachelor or a widower (1 Corinthians 7:8 is ambiguous).

Of course, Peter is dealing with marriage rather than ministry, though his entire agreement with Paul on this and his definition of Paul's letters as "Scriptures," (2 Peter 3:16) make it highly unlikely that they would not have been of the same mind on church roles as well.

The crucial passage (1 Peter 3:1–7) *could* be said to apply only to those marriages where the husband is an unbeliever—in which case his counsel to "submit" and "obey" *could* be seen as a relative tactic (to bring the husband round to a sympathetic attitude) rather than an absolute strategy (for all marriages, including those of two believers). But this is highly unlikely in view of the following:

1. The phrase "*if any* of them do not believe" clearly indicates that the command to "be submissive" also applies to wives with believing husbands.
2. The patriarchs' wives, who were certainly married to believers, are used as models.
3. The passage ends with a command to believing husbands.

Peter, like Paul, tells wives to "submit" to their husbands, but *never* tells husbands to "submit" to their wives. Both lay *other* responsibilities on the husband—to be considerate and treat with respect (1 Peter 3:7), to love, care, and cleanse (Ephesians 5:25–28). Peter's language goes somewhat further than Paul's; he commends Sarah for calling Abraham "Lord" (*kurion;* NIV softens this to "master") and giving him the obedience due to someone deserving that title.

His main point is that the best way for a wife to convert her husband is to change herself! She must not *tell* him what she thinks he should be or do; rather, she must become more attractive to look at and more attractive to live with (both will result from a right inner attitude to the husband). What is significant in this counsel is that the model for *Christian* wives is taken from the patriarchal period of the Old Testament.

The original paradox of Genesis 1 and 2 reappears in Peter's final exhortation to Christian husbands. Wives are the "weaker partner" (though he leaves the weakness undefined), and this "inequality" demands respect, not contempt; but they are equal *coheirs* of eternal life, which is a further ground for respect. Different in this world, they will be the same when the kingdom is finally and fully inherited (Matthew 25:34).

CHAPTER 5

COME BACK, PAUL

So, finally, we come to Paul. In the light of the last paragraph in the previous chapter, it is entirely appropriate to begin with his clearest statement that men and women are together heirs of the promised inheritance. But there is an even stronger reason for starting our study with Galatians 3:28. No text has been more quoted in relation to the issue under discussion. No text has been made to carry so much significance; it is often accorded similar significance to the Magna Carta or the Declaration of Independence! It is quoted as the last word on the subject. It has even been used *against* Paul himself, claiming that this was his highest inspiration and his other teaching represents a reversion to his preconversion, rabbinic prejudice!

If ever a text was used out of context as a pretext, this is it! If "neither male nor female" means that Christianity recognizes *no differences* in nature between men and women, then their roles are totally interchangeable in marriage (what could be wrong with a loving homosexual relationship?) and in ministry (presiding elder, archbishop, or pope!). This text cries out for careful *exegesis* (reading only what was originally in it) rather than casual *eisegesis* (reading other things into it).

In seeking the true meaning and application of this crucial verse, we must note the following points:

1. The whole letter deals with two dangers in Galatia—on the one hand, building faith on the law of Moses (focused in circumcision) rather than the promise of Abraham; on the other, interpreting liberty of the Spirit as license for the flesh. Since these twin errors erode the very foundation of our standing with God, the epistle is primarily concerned with the *vertical* spiritual relationship between God and man rather than the *horizontal* social relationships among human beings.

2. The immediate context (chapter 3) has *no* reference to the roles or relationships of men and women (nor are they mentioned anywhere else in the whole letter).

3. The theme is the inheritance of the blessing promised to Abraham and his "seed" (singular *spermati*, indicating "one," *enos* male, free descendant). It could not be inherited by a slave (Ishmael) or a girl or a Gentile.

4. Jesus fulfills the conditions and is the obvious son and heir—but how can anyone else (particularly a gentile slave women) possibly share the blessing with him?

5. The answer is simple: by total identification with Christ, anyone can claim the inheritance!

"Through faith *in* Christ Jesus" (verse 26), a person is "baptized *into* Christ" (verse 27), is "clothed *with* Christ" (verse 27), is "*in* Christ Jesus" (verse 28), and belongs "*to* Christ" (verse 29).

6. The literal translation of verse 28 is this: "There cannot be male *and* female, for all of you are one male in Christ Jesus." ("One" is masculine, not neuter; compare the "one new man" in Ephesians 2:15.)

7. So identification with Christ takes on *his* identity as that one free Jewish male descendant of Abraham—which qualifies *us* to inherit the promised blessing (of the Holy Spirit; see Galatians 3:14), which comes to us *through* Christ Jesus.

8. So *all* believers are *sons* in Christ. This could explain why the early church was always addressed *collectively* as "brothers," never as "brothers and sisters" (an *individual* believer was sometimes referred to as "sister" and there is one verse calling them "daughters," though this is a quotation from the Old Testament, 2 Corinthians 6:18 from 2 Samuel 7:8).

9. Because all are *sons*, then all are *heirs*, which daughters could never be (3:29).

10. So "in Christ" there is neither Jew nor Greek, only Jew; neither slave nor free, only free; not male and female, only male.

If this verse is taken out of its "inheritance" context and taken to abolish all sexual differences (i.e., in Christ we are virtually neutered), as well as social and racial distinctions, it would contradict Paul's teaching on homosexual relations (Romans 1:24–27; 1 Corinthians 6:9), on the duties of husbands and wives (Ephesians 5:22–23; Colossians 3:18–19), on slaves' attitude to their masters (Ephesians 6:5–9; Colossians 3:23–4:1), on God's future plans for Jewish people (Romans 11) and, in particular, on his qualifications of women's ministry in the church (1 Corinthians 11:3–16; 14:33–38; 1 Timothy 2:11–14), which we are about to consider. To accuse Paul of such inconsistency is a grave charge, with implications for the inspiration of Scripture as well as his personal integrity.

That Paul was not so careless in his thought is evidenced by an unnoticed but highly significant change in his language when dealing with the *horizontal* social relationships among believers. When he makes similar statements of principle in that context, *he omits the reference to male and female*. The most obvious example is Colossians 3:11, where he could hardly include the abolition of male and female in the context of teaching husbands and wives different duties. In fact, apart from Galatians 3:28, Paul nowhere included gender in such a statement (see Romans 3:22; 10:12; 1 Corinthians 12:13; Ephesians 2:15). Its *only* relevance is in the context of our inheritance in Christ. To enlarge one verse of Scripture into a social or an ecclesiastical manifesto is unwarranted and misleading, particularly in view of Paul's other specific teaching on the subject.

For it is with Paul that the paradox of gender comes to its clearest expression. The vertical equality of Genesis 1 is echoed in the sublime statement of Galatians

3:28 (the change from "neither . . . nor" to "not *male and female*" may indicate a direct reference). The horizontal inequality of Genesis 2 is actually quoted in such passages as 1 Corinthians 11 and 1 Timothy 2.

Not surprisingly, since paradox is offensive to logic even though it is often truer to life, many people have found Paul's position difficult and even inconsistent. Former generations failed to appreciate his emphasis on vertical equality. An age of egalitarian democracy is uncomfortable with his insistence on horizontal inequality. Feminists have hailed his statement in Galatians (expounded above) as the epitome of their inspiration—and hated him for almost everything else he said on the subject!

It has become fashionable to speak of the "problem passages" in the Pauline corpus. It should be noted that they are a "problem" only to those who have come to a different understanding of the total biblical context from that presented here. These texts are then seen as serious "misfits."

What's to be done with them? Until comparatively recently, there were only three possible attitudes to adopt.

1. *Paul was wrong then and is wrong now.* That is, he was *sincerely mistaken* in his views. Many liberal and a few evangelical scholars have pursued this line, claiming Paul's discrimination was more Jewish than Christian, a product of his rabbinic background.

Apart from the question this raises about the inspiration of Scripture (a serious issue for the true evangelical), such a view could be very unfair to Paul himself.

No rabbi ever encouraged a woman to *learn* anything (1 Timothy 2:11) and certainly never gave a woman conjugal rights over her husband's body (1 Corinthians 7:4). It is often in these very passages, which are regarded as so contentious, that Paul makes his strongest claims to be bringing revelation from Christ himself (1 Corinthians 14:37), to be accepted in all the churches (1 Corinthians 11:16). The onus of proof rests with those who reject his claims.

2. *Paul was right then but is wrong now.* That is, he was *culturally conditioned.* His counsel was only relevant to the social situation he was addressing; it is therefore relative rather than absolute, to be considered but not commanded in our very different circumstances.

There is an element of truth here: biblical truth revealed in one culture must be translated into another. It is the *principle* rather than the practice that is to be applied (footwashing? holy kissing?). Having said that, the baby can be thrown out with the bathwater! The principle can *include* the practice (bread eaten and wine drunk are vital parts of the "remembrance").

What we need is some *internal* indication in Scripture itself that cultural factors are operating. Yet what is so striking about Paul's teaching on gender is that he makes no reference to contemporary conditions (as he does on other issues, e.g., 1 Corinthians 7:26; 9:20–22). Instead, he specifically appeals to the original order of creation (1 Corinthians 11:8–9) and "the very nature of things" (1 Corinthians 11:14), both of which are constant criteria throughout history.

3. *Paul was right then and is right now.* That is, he was *divinely inspired* to set standards for all the churches and "for us, on whom the fulfillment of the ages has come." His principles apply throughout the "last days," which began at Pentecost.

Taken at face value and in their plainest meaning (a good Reformation hermeneutical principle), these passages do not allow women to be in a position of leading or directing men. The underlying principle is that the gender differences at the beginning of creation remain as a feature of the redeemed community. This is to be expressed both functionally (women are not to teach men) and visibly (men are to have "uncovered" heads and women "covered"). These requirements are totally consistent with the overall thrust of Scripture so far expounded in this book; indeed, they could be cut out of the canon, but the "problem" would remain.

However, there are those who believe these passages are utterly alien to the rest of Scripture, including the rest of Paul's teaching. They propose far more radical solutions to the "problem," adding two further attitudes.

4. *They are not Paul's message.* That is, they have been *added later.* The technical term is *interpolation.* Someone has been guilty of tampering with the text, introducing material of his own. The passages are fraudulent and must be ignored.

There is no doubt that this can happen and, indeed, has happened, even to manuscripts of the New Testament (an outstanding case was 1 John 5:7, a favorite text of Islamic critics of trinitarian Christianity, though it has been rightly excluded from translations since the Authorized King James Version). But there needs to be objective evidence (usually of a manuscript nature) before any particular passage is suspected. To dismiss texts simply because we may disagree with them or because we find it difficult to fit them into our hermeneutical scheme is to be similarly guilty of fraudulently handling Scripture.

5. *They are not Paul's meaning*. That is, they have been *translated badly*. This approach is increasingly popular among evangelical and charismatic feminists. If it is valid, many tensions could be resolved. But it involves the serious allegation that almost all previous translators of the Bible have been so culturally prejudiced that they have consciously or unconsciously distorted Paul's writings to the extent of making him say, in some cases, the exact opposite of what he intended! And it involves the implication that those making the proposed retranslation are sufficiently free of *today's* cultural conditioning to be objectively capable of discovering at last Paul's original meaning!

It takes a bit of swallowing, but needs to be taken seriously. The passages in question do have some grammatical and lexical ambiguities. And we can all be guilty of exegetical ventriloquism!

The remainder of this chapter will be given to the study of some of these key passages. The treatment cannot be exhaustive (the reader is referred to the many good commentaries). Only the major points of difference can be noted. Particular attention must be given to recent suggestions for retranslation or, in some cases, radical reinterpretation (the reader is asked to have at least one Bible translation at hand and, preferably, the Greek New Testament as well, if that is understood).

Before doing this, it is helpful to highlight the basic issue in the controversy over these texts. That is, does Paul teach a subordination based on gender (i.e., of women to men, what we have called the "horizontal inequality"), and is this part of God's word to us today?

Ephesians 5:21–33

The exhortation to *mutual* submission (in verse 21), formerly seen as the conclusion of the *preceding* section (see the paragraphs in the NIV, for example), is now said to be the introduction to the *following* section, thereby inculcating husbands' submission to wives, as well as wives' to husbands. Neither is to be "head" in a directive manner (see notes below on 1 Corinthians 11).

The reason given for switching the direction of verse 21 is the indisputable fact that the verb *submit* is missing from verse 22, but is implicitly carried over from the previous sentence (verse 22 literally begins: "Wives to your husbands"). It is not usually made clear how far the mutual submission has to be taken forward. Does this mean that there is a sense in which parents should "submit" to children, masters to slaves? An egalitarian philosophy might welcome this.

However, it makes most sense to see verse 21 as a link between the two sections. The phrase "to one another" looks back to the *general* exhortations applied to all believers in Ephesus (cf. verse 19) and refers to that attitude of humility appropriate to spiritual maturity (Philippians 2:3–4). The verb *submit,* however, *is* taken forward by itself to introduce the next sections, which move from general *mutual* submission to particular *unilateral* submission in specific contexts (primarily "domestic" and in the "household" of that day).

The word *submit* is not applied to husbands, either here or anywhere else in the New Testament. Nor is there even a phrase for husbands that "assumes" the verb from verse 21 (such as, "Husbands to your wives"). Nor is it valid to remove all notions of direction from the concept of headship. The husband is to be head of his wife in exactly the same manner *as* Christ is head of the church. No one has ever suggested that the church is not subordinate to her head.

However, Paul rightly emphasizes the balancing obligation of the husband *also* to love his wife *as* Christ loved the church. He must develop as well as direct, love as well as lead, sanctify as well as superintend, give himself as well as guide her. Few wives would be frustrated with such a husband!

Having said all this, the one difference in responsibility is clear. In the *one* flesh of marriage, the husband is the one "head" (verse 23), and the wife is the one "body" (verse 28), just as Christ is the head and the church his body. Marriage is to be neither a dictatorship nor a democracy!

1 Corinthians 11:2–16

The attempt to restate this passage is more complex,

beginning with the meaning of individual words. The key word is obviously *head*, which alternates between the literal (the top part of a human body) and the metaphorical. The latter reference is now said to refer to the "source" (as in head of river) rather than the "director" (as in head of school or head of state); in other words, it is to be emptied of any connotation of governmental authority. The word normally translated "woman" must now be rendered "wife," excluding single women from any regulation (the strictures therefore refer to marriage rather than gender). Finally, "authority" means to have authority *over* others rather than being under another's authority (so the wife's head-covering signifies her own authority instead of any obligation).

These lexical changes make Paul the author of some extraordinary statements! Verse 3 now states that "God is the *source* from whom Christ is derived." To avoid the charge of a christological heresy condemned by the church centuries ago, advocates refer to the "eternal generation" or the "temporal incarnation" of the Son—though the relevance of all that to the length of hair in church is somewhat elusive! Verse 3 also now states that "man is the *source* of woman," though a later verse states that the *source* of every man since Adam has been woman (verse 12)! And if "woman" should be translated "wife," then verse 12 is saying that "husband is born of wife," as well as "wife came from husband"! And what is this intrinsic authority of a married woman, represented by her head-covering? Who is it over?

It is not unkind to accuse these revisers of creating

more problems than they solve. The biggest question they leave is: What is the connection between the metaphorical and literal uses of the word *head*, a link that is obviously the key to the whole passage? Some *spiritual* aspect of headship provides the theological justification for men and women having different *physical* headcoverings. The traditional understanding of headship as including governmental responsibility (as in Ephesians 5:22–24) provides the connection and makes most sense of Paul's argument. The word *head* may have been used in the sense of "source" in classical Greek, but its biblical use is invariably hierarchical and governmental. The Greek Septuagint version of the Old Testament clearly does so (Deuteronomy 28:13; Judges 11:11; Isaiah 7:8), and this definition makes most sense of the New Testament usage as well (Ephesians 1:10, 22; Colossians 2:10).

There can be legitimate debate about the *form* of head-covering and how far the application needs to be adapted to other cultures. It is highly unlikely that Christian women used a veil (i.e., over the face), any more than Jewish women did. The choice seems to be between using something like a head-shawl (*not* one of the millinery marvels of today!) and simply wearing long hair, perhaps fastened up on the crown of the head. (The NIV margin gives the following rendering: "⁴Every man who prays or prophesies with long hair dishonors his head. ⁵And every woman who prays or prophesies with no covering of hair on her head dishonors her head—she is just like one of the 'shorn women.' ⁶If a woman has no covering, let her be for now with short hair, but since it is a disgrace for a woman to have her hair shorn or shaved, she should grow it again. [7]A man ought not to have long hair." This rendering omits all reference to veils. Actually, the Greek text uses it only once, in verse 15: "For long hair is given to her *instead* of a veil.")

The *principle* is quite clear, however. Gender must not be confused in gathering for worship. It is offensive to God (this is why homosexuality and transvestism are "abominations" to him) and is of significance (we are not told what) to the angels (verse 10), who also attend our services. The gender difference is to be visibly acknowledged (the sex of a worshiper should be perfectly obvious to a person in the pew behind!). For the woman, this expresses her acceptance of male governmental responsibility within the assembly, even while she participates freely in prayer and prophecy. For the man, it expresses his acknowledgment of the need to submit to the authority of Christ while he fulfills his role in church.

The crucial point to note is that Paul appeals to the original order of creation, to the "very nature of things," and to the universal practice of the churches; but he never mentions the social conditions in Corinth or the national culture of Greece. Enough said!

1 Corinthians 14:33–38

It would be foolish to deny that this is a "difficult" passage (even to understand, never mind integrate). The writer confesses to having found no fully satisfying exposition, but is comforted by the fact that no one else has either!

One of the best evangelical scholars feels it necessary to dismiss verses 34 and 35 as a later interpolation, though he has no reason for doing so apart from their inherent obscurity.

A less desperate, but still radical, "solution" treats these two verses as the statements of a Corinthian church leader claiming to have had a special revelation of strong sexist nature—which Paul is simply quoting before correcting (as in Romans 6:1 or 1 Corinthians 15:29). But there is nothing in the text to indicate this, and it doesn't really clarify anything.

One point that has teased scholars is the reference to what "the Law" says about women's submission. This would normally indicate Mosaic legislation, but the absence of any explicit command to this effect in the Sinaitic corpus has led some to postulate an "unknown" regulation in Greek society, which the apostle is quoting to support his position. Bibles with marginal references usually point to Genesis 3:16, but it is far more likely that Paul is drawing the same general conclusion from Genesis 2 that is outlined in the first chapter of this book (that woman was made *from*, *for*, and *after* man and was therefore *named* by him). Remember, "the Law" for Paul was the Pentateuch (all the first five books of the Bible). However, in a passage with a similar thrust, he quotes Genesis 2 *and* 3 (1 Timothy 2:13–14).

Can we approach the problem by considering the injunction of silence addressed to the women, bearing in mind the general understanding of male and female roles already reached?

If it is taken as a *total* ban on all verbal participation in worship gatherings, this passage is in direct contradiction (not just paradoxical tension!) to the praying and prophesying by women in 1 Corinthians 11:5 and even to the "everyone" in verse 26 of this very chapter.

In contrast to this wide application, others have narrowed it down to the prohibition of chatter and gossip among the women (assuming, doubtfully, that they sat separately from the men—though this is in a Christian fellowship, not a Jewish synagogue). But why should this not apply to the men also who are not above engaging in the same activity? That would be sexual discrimination of an offensive kind! Unhelpful talk is just as wrong in men (Ephesians 4:29), though it is a particular temptation for leisured women (1 Timothy 5:13).

Clearly, the particular application must lie between these two extremes. The immediate context is the matter of uncontrolled prophecy leading to disorder, and uncontrolled tongues before that. Both are individual and vocal contributions. Both need private and public constraints if the assembly is to know the order and peace of God. Does the injunction apply to the discussion about, or even the discipline of, such contributions? A rationale could be developed to distinguish between giving a prophecy (which involves no human authority, the message simply being passed on) and weighing, judging, and applying it (which does involve telling others what to do). That is, women may deliver prophecies but not debate them.

However, the reference seems a little wider than that, since women are told to satisfy their curiosity at home rather than in church. This covers more general discussions than simply weighing prophecy. Much as we may dislike it, Paul is apparently *excluding women from dialogue with teachers* in a church gathering, even to simply asking questions! Husbands are the right ones to engage in such dialogue, and that should be done in the private context of the home (what a challenge this presents to a husband, who must be *able* to answer his wife's questions; so often today it is the other way around!).

However much this conclusion outrages the modern mind, its likelihood is confirmed by a clearer statement of Paul's to the same effect: "A woman should learn in quietness and full submission." But we are jumping ahead to the last passage to be considered.

1 Timothy 2:11–15

This is widely considered to be the passage most offensive to Christian women in the writings of Paul, if not the whole New Testament. It has certainly drawn the most feminist fire, for it apparently imposes severe limitations on their public ministry and perpetuates a male-dominated church.

Not surprisingly, these verses are now being retranslated in the most radical manner. Maybe the simplest way to present all the proposed revisions would be to include them in a complete paraphrase:

Verse 11: You must teach women so that they can become teachers themselves; as with men under instruction, the women also must not interrupt with aggressive opinions of their own.

Verse 12: Personally, I don't make a practice of letting women teach because hitherto they have not had the educational opportunity to study the Scriptures; asserting their somewhat ignorant ideas in an authoritarian manner could be seen as putting down their husbands.

Verse 13: Nevertheless, when Adam was created, he was immediately given a colleague to complete and complement him as a coequal, sharing fully his dual role of ruling the world and teaching others the word of God.

Verse 14: Satan was able to deceive Eve only because she was not personally present when God spoke to Adam and she had only a second-hand report of what was said; Adam, on the other hand, knew better and his sin, unlike hers, was inexcusable.

Verse 15: This is why God spoke so tenderly to Eve, promising to vindicate her innocence and save her from undeserved dishonor and shame by choosing a woman to bear that special Child who would defeat Satan and thus save all women of faith, love, holiness, and good sense.

This paraphrase is entirely composed of the new

translations and interpretations proposed by evangelical and charismatic leaders who have embraced the cause of Christian feminism.

It could be called the "Reversed Version," for the meaning of each verse is almost the opposite of that understood by former translators and expositors. The basic changes may be listed thus:

Verse 11: This imperative to "learn" has become a command to teach and has been altogether separated from the qualifying phrase "in quietness and full submission," which is now applied to both sexes.

Verse 12: Paul's prohibition is relativized by relating it to educational opportunity (with obvious implications for today!). The *two* prohibitions ("to teach *or* to have authority") have been rolled into one ("teach in an authoritarian manner"), thus neutralizing the second.

Verse 13: "First" no longer carries any sense of priority, seniority, or responsibility and is therefore now an obsolete word. The emphasis is on the simultaneous rather than the successive creation of Adam and Eve.

Verse 14: Eve is now entirely innocent, deserving comfort and vindication rather than punishment for her part in the Fall.

Verse 15: "Childbearing" is applied exclusively to one woman: Mary.

Where does one begin (or end!) in dealing with such a complex revision of Scripture? It is frustrating that

Paul himself is not available to give us his own opinion about what he is purported to have meant to say! He would probably be astonished, then indignant.

Those who have a working knowledge of Greek have the advantage of checking whether the "Reversed Version" is true to the grammar and syntax of the original text. They will probably get no further than verse 11 before they have serious doubts about the objectivity, and even integrity, of the "new" translators. For example, "in quietness and full submission" is integral to the imperative verb and clearly refers to "woman"; the sentence cannot be separated into *two* commands. It is not about *who* men must teach but about *how* women must learn!

However, many readers will not have the technical expertise to check the plausible justification advanced for this radical revision. Who are they to believe? The problem is complicated when those proposing the changes are widely respected for their attitudes and abilities in other areas.

One simple approach is to read as many "accepted" translations as possible—both those done by groups of scholars (King James Version, Revised Version, Revised Standard Version, New English Bible, New International Version, American Standard Version, New American Standard Bible, Jerusalem Bible, Amplified Bible, New King James Version, etc.) and those done by individual translators (Today's English Version, Living Bible, Phillips, Moffatt, Knox, Weymouth, etc.). The first thing that strikes the reader is the astonishing unanimity of *all* the translators concerning the meaning of the Greek text. They might have disagreed *with* what Paul said; but never *about* what he said!

To believe that all of them were the victims of blind prejudice, projecting their own chauvinism and obscuring Paul's feminism, stretches credulity beyond its normal limits. It also borders on libel, questioning as it does the ability and integrity of many men of God.

However, the average Bible reader need not limit his judgment to this kind of comparison. "Common people" are capable of shrewd insight and sound thinking (Mark 12:37). Any translation may be meditated upon as well as read. This profitable privilege of "private interpretation" of Scripture was a Reformation rediscovery.

For example, let the reader think through this recent claim that Paul prohibited women from teaching only because of their educational disadvantages in his own day. The following questions will soon spring to mind:

- Why doesn't Paul explicitly give this as the reason?
- Was this as true in gentile society as in Jewish?
- Were there no educated women? (Lydia? Priscilla?)
- Did Paul forbid uneducated men to teach?
- Weren't most Christian men uneducated? (1 Corinthians 1:26)
- Didn't Timothy get his knowledge of Scripture from his mother and grandmother? (2 Timothy 1:5; 3:15)
- Why does Paul appeal to Genesis 2 and 3?
- How does this fit in with his other teaching? (1 Corinthians 14:34)

- Does it apply to uneducated women (or men) today?

It will become apparent that Paul's prohibition relates to gender, not ignorance, and that this is based on creation, not culture. Above all, the reader will probably conclude that a gift for teaching Christians requires spiritual rather than intellectual qualifications and is often quite unrelated to academic ability or opportunity.

It is time to look more positively at the passage as it has been normally understood and accepted. Let us do justice to Paul by listening to him, whether we find it easy or hard to agree with him. What does he really say?

We have to accept that there *is* discrimination between the sexes here (if and when the exemption of churches from the [British] Sex Discrimination Act is removed, as it may well be, Christians following Paul's teaching will be liable to prosecution!). Limitations are imposed on women's participation in the activities of the church for no other reason than their gender. There are three limits, two specific and one general.

First, when *public* teaching is taking place, women are to accept it without answering back or even asking questions (cf. 1 Corinthians 14:34–35). The modesty expressed in dress and adornment (1 Timothy 2:9) must extend to their learning attitudes also. Debate and dialogue are to be left to the men. Before uttering cries of outrage ("What will happen to our house groups?"), we need to pause and remember that Jewish rabbis wouldn't even let a woman *learn* at all (though they had no Scripture for this). Paul is taking a Christian, not a Jewish, position in teaching both sexes (as Jesus did before him).

Second, women are not to teach at all in the mixed congregation (Titus 2:3 shows he encouraged them to do this on other occasions when men were not present). To expand this, we perhaps need to understand that in those days "preaching" was primarily announcing the gospel to unbelievers, whereas "teaching" was addressed to believers (*most* of what we call "preaching," i.e., "pulpiteering," is, in New Testament terminology, "teaching").

Third, the *general* prohibition in verse 12 is at the heart of the passage and covers much more than learning or teaching. The usual word translated "to usurp authority" could be used of physical violence, but things hadn't gotten that bad in the early church! Its other meaning is nearer to the colloquial English expressions of "lecturing" someone, "laying down the law," and "lording it over" others. In simple terms, it means directing someone in a way inappropriate to the relationship (as in "Don't *you* tell *me* what to do!"—an expression conveying very clearly the emotional undertones of the Greek word). For a woman to direct a man is an act of "violence"; it violates the order of creation.

That is the ground on which Paul bases the three prohibitions. They express quite literally the "order" in which Adam and Eve were created (verse 13). A further reason is to be found in Eve's part in the Fall, in which she "was deceived" and "became a sinner." Her assuming the role of leadership had disastrous consequences and must not be followed by other women.

One consequence was the increased pain (and, therefore, risk) of childbirth. Paul ends the section, which has been wholly addressed to women, with a word of comfort that a continued state of faith, love, holiness, and modesty will save them through childbearing. The question is, "saved" from what? The simplest answer is danger and death. It cannot mean that she will be saved from sin and hell *by* having children (though a midwife told the author that many mothers turn toward God when they are in labor!), though some commentators take it that women will find their true fulfillment and wholeness in having and leading children rather than trying to lead men (influencing the human race from the bottom rather than the top).

At any rate, Paul finishes on a positive note. It is therefore fitting that we should do the same in this chapter on his teaching.

He excludes women from any activity involving the *leadership* of men, but he encourages women in many forms of *ministry*. Though his qualifications for eldership are male ("husband of one wife . . . able to manage his own family well" [1 Timothy 3:2–4]), the ministry of deacons is open to all (this is more likely to be the meaning of "women" in 1 Timothy 3:11, the very next chapter, and is confirmed by the "deaconess" Phoebe in Romans 16:1). The whole chapter 16 in Romans is an eye-opener to those who have thought of Paul as a woman hater! A third of those he commends are women, who have acquitted themselves more than manfully (sorry!) in the work of the Lord. They bear the title "fellow worker," *colleagues* of Paul (as were Euodia and Syntyche in Philippians 4:2), which means they shared in his mission of evangelism and church-planting. We know from the Epistles that wives accompanied apostles on their travels (1 Corinthians 9:5; they had to be believers!). If women were part of an apostolic team (led by men, of course!), that would explain why Junia (almost certainly a feminine name, though this cannot be proved; see Romans 16:7 [KJV]) is counted among the apostles (remembering that this word, meaning "sent one," applies to anyone going somewhere else on someone's behalf, hence the application of Epaphroditus, "sent" to Rome to be Paul's house-keeper, in Philippians 2:25). Paul even enjoyed being "mothered" (Romans 16:13), which may come as a surprise. But he kept his kisses "holy"!

And his overall objective was positive—that both men and women should have the *right* attitudes to one another and engage in the *right* activities appropriate to their gender. This is what *right*eousness is all about.

CHAPTER 6

...AND EVER
SHALL BE?

No biblical survey of any subject would be complete without a glimpse into the future. Will the paradox of gender continue into the new heaven and new earth, the final age of the kingdom of God?

The clearest pointer we have is the statement of Jesus that in the next life men will not marry and women will not be given in marriage (Matthew 22:30). Human beings will be "like the angels." At the *physical* level, marriage will not be necessary for reproduction or multiplication, since death will be no more. At the *spiritual* level, the analogy (between the male/female and divine/human relationships, as outlined in the first chapter) will no longer be needed, since we shall know even as we have been known (1 Corinthians 13:12).

This does not necessarily mean that our new bodies will be sexless, even in appearance ("bits having dropped off," as one charismatic leader put it!). The angels, whom we shall resemble, are not necessarily neuter beings. Usually described as masculine (Genesis 18:2), they may sometimes be feminine (Zechariah 5:9).

They may even be capable of intercourse with and impregnation of human beings, if Genesis 6:2 is correctly linked with Jude 6 through the apocryphal book of Enoch. In any case our bodies will be like the glorious body of the risen, ascended Jesus, which presumably has not lost its gender or full complement of organs.

The New Jerusalem will have the names of twenty-four Jewish *men* on the gates and foundations (will they be the "twenty-four elders"?). Both the city and its people are seen in bridal terms (Revelation 21:2; 22:17).

The answer to most of our speculative questions is that we neither know nor need to know. One thing is clear, however. We cannot live in *this* world as if we were already in the *next*, at least in the area of our sexuality. Otherwise, we would fall into the heresy of asceticism, preaching celibacy as a superior state to marriage (see 1 Corinthians 7:29; 1 Timothy 4:3). Paul commended celibacy for temporal rather than eternal reasons (1 Corinthians 7:26). For exactly the same reasons, the roles and relationships between male and female must balance our hopes for the next world with our circumstances in this world (1 Peter 3:7 gets it right!). The present differences between the sexes must be recognized and respected precisely *because* they will one day disappear.

Turning from this biblical survey to the contemporary scene, we have to ask, What is the Spirit saying to the churches? An increasing number of charismatic leaders believe he is telling us that leadership of the church can be equally male or female. How can such a far-reaching claim be adequately judged? At least five tests spring to mind.

1. Is it true to *Scripture?* The preceding chapters have raised very serious questions on this score, in relation to both the general tenor and the particular statements of the Old and New Testaments. The Spirit is not likely to cancel or contradict the Scriptures he himself inspired! It is in this very context of gender relationships that we are exhorted not to "malign the word of God" (Titus 2:5) and not to imagine the word of God originated with us (1 Corinthians 14:36).

2. Are there clear and tested *prophecies?* And are these coming through reliable channels, devoid of vested interest? Jack Hayford reports the specific word he received about *men:* "Begin to meet with the *men* and I will raise up elders and servants to accomplish my purpose here" *(The Church on the Way).* Have there been such specific and confirmed revelations directly linking women with responsible leadership?

3. Are human *emotions* tending to influence discernment? Certainly this is a highly emotive issue. There is often frustration and sometimes anger on the women's side; often guilt and sometimes fear on the men's. Churches have been male-dominated rather than male-directed, with suppressed rather than expressed womanhood. But subjective reaction to one wrong can so easily swing the pendulum to an opposite extreme. It takes a clear mind and a cool heart to remain objective.

4. *Who else* supports the revelation? The Holy Spirit has not given charismatics a monopoly on truth. He

can speak through anyone (even Balaam's ass!), either inside or outside the church. Nevertheless, his prophetic direction is not usually in line with the world's thinking or even with the whole spectrum of the church's theology. Yet on this issue of women's liberation into *leadership,* charismatics are joined by other evangelicals, by liberals, and by radicals. And secular humanists are shouting the message louder than any of them. Such a broad climate of opinion makes it vital to discern between the leading of the Holy Spirit and the pressure of the "spirit" of the age! We need to remember that the world cannot receive the Spirit of truth, neither seeing nor knowing him (John 14:17). His guidance is not necessarily in conflict with public opinion, but the two are not often in harmony. Popular consensus is an unreliable barometer (Luke 6:26).

5. Could *Satan* benefit from it? He is the original vandal, finding pleasure in destroying what God has created. He is determined to break up marriages (which are based on difference of gender; see Genesis 2:24) and families (which are rooted in paternalism; see Ephesians 3:15). Contrary to widespread delusion, God is *for* sex (it was his idea!), and Satan is *against* sex. Through unisex and homosex, the devil is separating sex from gender, the physical from the social. He knows this will weaken authority in the home—as it also will in the church. He has encouraged unilateral independence from the beginning. The confusion of identity in contemporary society has his stamp on it (some of the most complex pastoral needs this writer has encountered concerned persons who had already had or were

seeking a sex change). It would be ironic if a church abolishing sex distinction was actually doing the devil's work for him!

These five tests and the comments made on them are not conclusive. At the very least, however, they indicate the need for extreme caution in the discussion, and even more in the application, of the matter. Unfortunately, the issue can be clouded by presenting it in misleading terms of reference, as the following examples demonstrate.

It is not a *clerical* issue. To focus on the ordination of women is misleading unless the ordination of men is also questioned. There is no *New* Testament warrant for a sacerdotal monopoly of dispensing sacraments by men (or women) and no limiting of priesthood to one gender. The real issue is whether *any* ordination puts a woman in a position "over" men. The Catholic (Anglo and Roman) objection to ordaining women does not rest on apostolic doctrine. Neither does the division of the people of God into clergy and laity, minister and members, pulpit and pew. These ecclesiastical traditions, based on the old covenant rather than the new, only confuse the debate.

It is not a *hierarchical* issue. In this approach, leadership is seen as a ladder, and the debate centers on how far up women are allowed to climb. The line is drawn at various levels—vicar, but not bishop; house group leader, but not elder; team member, but not team leader; and so on. One variation of this "solution" is to reserve only the very top rung for *men* (or, more usually, one man); as long as the archbishop (in house church jargon "apostle") is male, any lower ranks may be female. Not only is it difficult to find biblical justification for where the line is drawn; it is almost impossible to justify the ladder of hierarchy (Jesus taught a "lower-archy"; see Matthew 20:25–28; 1 Peter 5:3). The real issue is whether *at any level* (house group to Vatican council) the relationship between the sexes is as God intended it to be.

It is not a *situational* issue. The shortage of men on the mission field, the unavailability of men to do pastoral work in Korea, the dearth of strong men in English churches—none of these can justify the use of women in leadership. Indeed, it is an insult to women to use them only because men are not available, with the implication of their redundancy if and when men were available! Before circumstances force us into such patterns of expediency, we must first be sure of the principles involved—particularly the question of whether sex distinction is relative or absolute, a product of culture or creation.

It is not a *historical* issue. Church history is a mixed bag. It is predominantly chauvinist, but there are also many examples of feminine leadership, particularly, though not exclusively, in the last century and this (the era of the social emancipation of women as well). However, the evangelical is not persuaded by the precedent of tradition (either way!), any more than the Reformers were. The church(es) can be wrong; the Bible, rightly interpreted, cannot be.

It is not an *experimental* issue. A pragmatic age is more concerned with whether it works than whether it is right. In Christian jargon the pragmatist asks, Is it blessed? That God has blessed women's leadership cannot be denied; that this proves it is right may be debated. God does not wait till we are perfect before he blesses (who would be blessed if he did?); the gracious doctrine of justification by faith means that he treats us *already* as if we were all right in his sight. Furthermore, God is above the rules he makes for us and is perfectly free to make exceptions for himself, as long as they are consistent with himself (miracles in nature are an example of his liberty). His blessing on Salvation Army women in no way implies his approval of a military structure or his indifference to the sacraments. His gracious activity needs the confirmation of Scripture before it can be taken as a sanction (a good example of this principle may be found in Acts 15).

These five aspects are relevant and need to be aired; but none of them provides the proper starting point.

It is essentially a *biblical* issue, to be settled by scrupulous exegesis. That is why the major portion of this book has been devoted to a scriptural survey that, though far from comprehensive or adequate, has sought to expose the overall thrust of Scripture as well as its contributory elements. The conclusion drawn is that the paradox of gender in creation (the vertical equality and the horizontal inequality) remains a feature of life in this present world and is consistently maintained throughout the Old and New Testaments.

It then becomes a *practical* issue. Once biblical convictions have been reached, they have to be applied within the situations in which we find ourselves. It seems appropriate to conclude with an outline of the practical implications of the conclusion reached. There are three obvious applications, one negative and two positive.

In regard to the *negative* application, we must stop putting women in positions of leadership over men.

In the *church*, the Scripture clearly applies this prohibition to eldership and teaching (in a mixed congregation). The more complex programs of church activity today demand careful examination of other forms of leadership (worship, choirs, house groups, and evangelistic teams, for example). The guideline must be function rather than office, relationship rather than title, responsibility rather than status. Does the position foster unbiblical roles?

The principle extends from the church to the *home*, for these two units in God's redemptive society are profoundly related, though never totally identified. The common practice of evangelizing and edifying wives apart from their husbands must be challenged. When a wife is spiritually *ahead* of her husband, it is increasingly difficult for her to regard him as *the head*. The church has created many "unequal yokes" in this way, making possible the breakdown of marriage (1 Corinthians 7:15). Husband and wife should be treated as *one* flesh, whether neither, either, or both are unbelievers. An unbelieving husband is head of his house (should his wife be admitted to membership or given responsibility in the church unless he expressly desires it?). Without intending, or even realizing it, Christians have often encouraged wives to become spiritual leaders to their husbands (see the suggestion below for a needed correction of this trend).

There are two major *positive* applications, one for women and one for men.

For the WOMEN, more opportunities of ministry need to be opened up. It is often frustration over the lack of these that has led to a demand for shared leadership. Many Christian women who accept that biblical leadership is male rightly complain that avenues of ministry have been unnecessarily inhibited by male monopoly. The charge is often justified. The variety and the scope of women's ministry are outside the range of this book, which is exclusively concerned with the issue of leadership. However, the writer is convinced there are many more to be explored than is customary, which do not in any way involve the direction of men.

The church has need of spiritual mothers as well as fathers (Romans 16:13). As they recover their special mission to the poor, women will be seen to be more suitable than men for works of mercy (Proverbs 31:20; Acts 9:36), which will be increasingly needed as governmental assistance programs fail. The public ministries of praying and prophesying are particularly effective when exercised by women of spiritual insight and sensitivity.

In short, the work of the kingdom needs both men and women as fellow workers with each other (Romans 16:3) and with God. Christian women are capable of working very hard in the Lord (cf. Mary, Tryphena, Tryphosa, and Persis in Romans 16; none of the men receive this accolade!). They should be given every possible opportunity of gaining their reward in heaven. Their selfless, sacrificial, and often secret service is a special delight to the Lord.

For the MEN, more training for leadership needs to be given. The answer to the present imbalance is not to weaken the women's contribution but to strengthen the men's! Local churches must give top priority to evangelizing and discipling *men*, as Jesus did. His investment of time and teaching in a handful of men (most of whom were skilled manual workers) laid the right foundation for a church that would experience spectacular growth. It is better to teach a man to lead his wife and family than to provide women's meetings and youth clubs to compensate for a godless father.

Jack Hayford's example in *The Church on the Way* could be profitably followed by most pastors: "Meet with the *men.*" In many countries men have to leave their families and jobs for a time of military training each year so that they can defend their homes, communities, and nation against an enemy. The author has a vision for a very large gathering of men in such a spiritual training camp to encourage them to be leaders in their families, churches, employment, communities, and the nation itself. Interest is spreading and enthusiasm growing. It would be utterly wrong to deny leadership to women and do little or nothing about training men for this responsibility.

Working all this out in our local churches and national cultures requires great wisdom. This book has deliberately refrained from detailed application. *Direction* comes from the Scripture, but *directions* come from the Spirit. The Word tells us *where* to go; wisdom tells us *how* to get there. This final chapter has attempted to ask the right questions but not to give the final answers. The author hopes that the reader is left in the creative tension between what *is* and what *ought to be* that highlights the need of the body for the Head, the bride for the Bridegroom. Only in direct dependence on the Lord Jesus Christ and through the direct guidance of the Holy Spirit can the will of God be done on earth.

CONCLUSION

The role of women in the church was already head-line news when my book first appeared in England. The vigorous response to the publication of my views in that edition has helped to clarify my own thinking, if no one else's! What has been the result?

I now wish to correct a few details of exegesis (for example, it has been rightly pointed out that Mary as well as Joseph was given the responsibility of naming Jesus; cf. Luke 1:31 with Matthew 1:21). At other points, unintended ambiguity has led to a misunderstanding of my position (in stating that our resurrection bodies will be like the body of our glorified Lord "which presumably has not lost its gender," I did not mean to imply that we would all become male but that we will probably retain sexual differentiation.)

Above all, the debate has focused my attention on the real issues underlying our differences of opinion. Since I deliberately concentrated on an examination of the biblical data, which must be prior to social or ecclesiastical questions, these issues are related to the task of interpretation and the presuppositions we all bring to it.

There are three ways in which our basic convictions will be decisive—namely, our understanding of the nature of gender, the nature of Scripture, and the nature of God (I nearly said, "God himself," but that would prejudge the discussion!). In adding this conclusion, which explores these crucial subjects, I hope that some readers will be led from confusion to convictions.

The Nature of Gender

The basic question is this: What are the essential differences between men and women? Are they only physical, partly psychological, also sociological, or even spiritual?

The answer, whether we discover it inside or outside Scripture, will determine our interpretation of the two crucial texts relative to the role of men and women in home, church, and society. Indeed, the whole debate may be said to hinge on just two phrases, in the Old and New Testaments, respectively: "male and female" (Genesis 1:27) and "not male and female" (Galatians 3:28; literal translation).

1. "Male and female" (Genesis 1:27)

It is obvious that "man" *(adam)* in this verse refers to "mankind," genus rather than gender, "them" rather than "him" (as in Genesis 5:1–2). It is equally clear that God created two distinct types within the one species—

male and female. Exactly what distinguishes one from the other?

Is there a *spiritual* difference? Few Christians would read this into the phrase. Most would affirm that men and women are equal in the sight of God, both bearing his image, capable of fellowship with him, jointly responsible for obedience to him and dominion over his other creatures on earth.

Is there a *physical* difference? All Christians take this for granted. Even though the degree of sexual characteristics may vary (with hormones), the basic difference remains (in chromosomes).

Are there *psychological* differences (in makeup) and *sociological* ones (in function)? This is the key issue. There is no hint of an answer in Genesis 1, but from Genesis 2 onward the gender difference is clearly regarded with more than biological significance. From the male initiative in establishing marriage (Genesis 2:24) to the prohibition of transvestism (Deuteronomy 22:5), the Pentateuch contains clear social guidelines based on gender. Very few are prepared to argue that Old Testament society was any other than patriarchal in constitution

Furthermore, the tacit assumption that there are real differences between male and female attitudes and actions underlies most of the Wisdom Literature (the book of Proverbs in particular). On the rare occasions when God is said to act "like" a mother, the simile would lose its force if it does not imply "unlike" a father.

However, that does not settle the question; it merely leads on to another. Was the Jewish understanding of "male and female" as having social as well as sexual implications a matter of culture or creation, heredity or environment?

Some believe it was *relative*. That is, their outlook was culturally conditioned in a world where patriarchy was the norm. In this case, we are not only free to ignore the social patterns of the Old Testament; it becomes imperative that we abolish them and liberate women into their full personhood. Sexual differences are purely physical and must not be allowed to influence any other aspect of life, either individual or corporate.

Others (including myself) believe it was *absolute*. That is, there are real differences between men and women, both in their nature and in their relationships, which are rooted in the original creation and will be permanent features of a healthy society. Any attempt to obliterate these distinctions (even in the name of equality), whether through legal or social pressure, will in the long term damage our humanity, causing confusion (particularly crises of identity) and frustration (as we try to be what God never intended us to be). A unisex society is contrary to divine creation, not just Hebrew tradition.

Which viewpoint is taken in the New Testament? Increasingly, the claim is made that the covenant of Jesus has rendered obsolete all gender distinction other than physical. One text, and one phrase within it, has been made to carry the major responsibility for this radical change of view (I have already referred to the common practice of calling it the Magna Carta of Christian feminism). We will now examine it.

2. "Not male and female"
(Galatians 3:28; literal translation)

At first glance, this phrase is the exact opposite of the one we have just looked at. It could be taken to mean that people who are "in Christ" have ceased to be what they were in creation. Few dare to take the phrase so literally. Such an interpretation would run counter to the profound New Testament principle that redemption is the restoration of God's original creation, not its abolition. So to which differences between male and female does it apply?

Is the *spiritual* difference canceled? But we have already seen that it never did apply. The whole context of Galatians 3 is a concern about who can inherit the spiritual blessing (and, in particular, the Holy Spirit) promised to Abraham and his "seed" (singular). The answer is now—anybody can, provided the person is "in Christ." The "not" does not indicate any change from Genesis 1, but simply that what was formerly limited to one free male Jew is now available to all, regardless of race, class, or gender.

Is the *physical* difference canceled? If "in Christ" we are now to be regarded as biologically neutered, then it is legitimate for Christians to enter into homosexual unions or even seek a sex change! However, not many would be prepared to argue that the second birth has such a radical effect on sexuality.

Are any *psychological* or *sociological* differences canceled? This is the heart of the matter. Our views will depend on whether we regard these differences as relative or absolute (see above). To put it more theologically, are these differences the result of the Fall in Genesis 3, or do they belong to the "innocence" of Genesis 2? If the former, we need to be redeemed from them; if the latter, they need to be restored. If (as I believe) they are a mixture of both, we need to discern which is which and restore valid differences to their sin-free state.

Neither the verse nor its context supplies any guidelines for this exercise (hardly surprising, since Paul was here dealing with a purely spiritual issue and not directly considering any sexual or social outworking of it). So we must look elsewhere in the New Testament to see how the principle of Galatians 3:28 was worked out in practice. To put it simply, do the apostolic writers assume that all differences between male and female (other than the physical) have been abolished "in Christ"?

Clearly, they do not! Both Peter and Paul assign different roles and responsibilities to husbands and wives, particularly toward their partners. Paul prohibits women *as women* from some functions within the church (certainly teaching, probably eldership, and possibly discussion of doctrine or prophecy). While encouraging women to pray and prophesy, he insists that their gender be acknowledged in their coiffure. Significantly, all these contexts refer to Genesis and especially to chapter 2.

If these "apostolic doctrines" are taken at face value,

we may conclude that "male and female" in Genesis 1:27 and "not male and female" in Galatians 3:28 are, in fact, fully compatible and not in any way contradictory. Both in creation and "in Christ," there are no spiritual differences, clear physical differences, and some psychological/sociological differences. The latter have not become obsolete—though it must be said that there are fewer under the new covenant than under the old (reflecting the fuller redemption from those differences that were the result of the Fall; cf. Matthew 19:8).

However, many modern Christians are not content with the New Testament *reduction* of social distinctions (to the outlook of an egalitarian age, the remaining ones are still regarded as discrimination). They insist on the abolition of *all* such limitations, including those apparently advocated by the apostles. Texts containing these are now labeled as "problem passages"! The way they are handled brings us to the second major issue of interpretation.

The Nature of Scripture

It is only when we find something difficult or disagreeable in the Bible that we discover our real understanding of the inspiration and authority of Scripture. It is possible to believe in neither and still freely quote the Bible to support one's case (even Satan did so!). It is what we do with passages that contradict our convictions that reveals whether we consider ourselves "above" or "below" Scripture, judges of it or judged by it.

This may be readily illustrated by the way these Petrine and Pauline "problem passages" have been handled, especially in the attempt to align them with an understanding of Galatians 3:28 that abolishes all gender distinctions of role. Broadly speaking, feminist theology has followed three lines of interpretation.

1. The *liberal* approach accepts neither the inspiration nor the authority of these passages. Invariably, the technique is to have "a canon within the canon" by selecting some parts of Scripture (usually in an arbitrary or a subjective manner according to reason, tradition, or even sentiment) and using this abstracted portion as a criterion for weighing and judging all other parts.

Thus, in the present case, Galatians 3:28 is accepted as a truly inspired utterance, and in its light Paul's other statements are judged to be uninspired and unfortunate "lapses," due to his misogynist temperament and/or rabbinic background. His "prejudiced opinions" may therefore be safely ignored in this enlightened age. The poor chap never quite lived up to his earliest ideal (assuming Galatians was his first epistle)!

A variant on this "uninspired" theme is the claim that the majority of scholars do not regard these passages as having come from the hand of Paul himself. This explanation asserts that later writers used his name as a cover for their own ideas (the technical term for such fraudulent forgeries is *pseudepigrapha*). This represents an attempt to acknowledge the authority of Paul's teaching, while rejecting the "problem passages" within his letters. There may be some ground for this assessment of 1 Timothy, but there is even less for

Ephesians and none at all for 1 Corinthians. However, if it were ever established that these were all from another hand (which is very far from proven), the fact remains that they have all been recognized by the church as having apostolic authority and therefore entitled to the respect accorded to holy Scripture.

2. The *liberal/evangelical* accepts the inspiration but not the authority of these passages. The argument is that the circumstances of those days made Paul's restrictions necessary, but our contemporary situation renders them irrelevant. Two versions of this are current.

On the one hand, the simpler explanation relates to the immoral culture of the ancient world, which required Christian women to guard against giving misleading impressions of their "liberty" in Christ (by immodest appearance or "forward" behavior). On the other hand, a more subtle explanation finds the reason in pagan cults, particularly of the Gnostic variety, and the place they gave to goddesses and priestesses. Either approach enables the "problem passages" to be treated as reactions (even overreactions) to the world rather than regulations for the church.

But the fact remains that none of the passages in question specifically mentions such cultures or cults. However, the main objection to this line of interpretation is that it assumes that our moral and spiritual conditions today are so greatly improved that these precautions are no longer necessary. Enough said!

3. The *evangelical* approach accepts both the inspiration and the authority of these passages. The only

matters open to discussion are whether the translations are true to the original and whether the interpretations are true to the text. Two schools of thought have emerged.

First, there are those who wish to *alter* the traditional translation and interpretation of these passages, believing they have grossly distorted Pauline doctrine. Appealing to both etymology (the derivation and meaning of words) and grammar (the construction of sentences and paragraphs), they propose a radical revision that removes all gender discrimination from the texts (I have already given details of this in chapter 5). The argument justifying this is not easy to follow and almost impossible to remember (two of its main proponents have candidly admitted that it requires "difficult, complex, and even convoluted exegesis"). The view credits the Lord with considerable carelessness over the transmission and translation of the inspired text. It is difficult to avoid the impression of a determination to combine feminist convictions with an evangelical reputation. The liberal disagreement with Paul seems more honest.

Second, there are those (including myself) who are willing to *accept* the approved translations and the traditional interpretation of them as truly representing Pauline doctrine. They follow the sound hermeneutical principle of taking Scripture in its plainest, simplest sense—unless otherwise indicated by the text itself. Instead of trying to make "awkward" texts fit into a preconceived system of thought, apparent contradictions are taken as different aspects of truth to be held together in dialectical or even paradoxical tension. Predestination and free will are the classic examples of this humble acceptance of the whole word of God. My book has sought to apply the same principle to the biblical paradox of the equality of male and female (in Genesis 1 and Galatians 3) and their inequality (in Genesis 2 and 1 Timothy 2).

In this connection, I was intrigued by the comments made by a highly critical reviewer (Bishop Richard Holloway in the *Church Times*) on the British edition of this book:

> In searching the Scriptures he can find only patriarchy or male leadership as the model for relationship between the sexes, and he is absolutely right. That's what the Bible says, along with a lot of other stuff we have long since discarded.
>
> Mr. Pawson's difficulty is tragic. He is a good and kindly man and a fine Christian leader, but he is absolutely hung up on a fundamentalist method of scriptural interpretation. It makes him consistent, or as consistent as Scripture; but he believes in doing what he thinks the Bible tells him to do.

Apart from the pejorative epithet *fundamentalist* (which now carries the connotation of an illiterate literalist), I take these remarks as a backhanded compliment and will save them for whoever has the thankless task of writing my epitaph!

Accepting Scripture as it stands, without addition, subtraction, or alteration, raises the final major issue of biblical interpretation in relation to this debate, which is covered in the next section.

The Nature of God

Evangelicals believe that God inspired the words of Scripture as well as the Word in Scripture. Not that the human authors were mere robots. But the Spirit so worked with and through them that their forms of expression were the best possible to communicate the revelation God wished to share with mankind. It follows from this premise that if we want to know what God is really like, we cannot improve on the language used by the biblical writers.

For example, they used a considerable amount of what is called "anthropomorphic" (from *anthropos*, "man," and *morphe*, "form") language, describing God as if he were human. The Bible speaks of his eyes, ears, mouth, nostrils, hand, arm—and even of his kidneys, bowels, and sperm! Yet the Bible clearly states he is spirit and therefore has no body. So why use such inappropriate terms? Because our abilities to see, hear, speak, smell, hold, hit, feel, and beget are the nearest things in our experience to the living God. Such terms foster an intensely personal concept of God, "like us" because we are "like him."

The alternative forms of expression proposed by those who consider themselves too sophisticated for such naivete invariably convey the impression of a deity who is impersonal rather than personal, static rather than dynamic, an object to be contemplated rather than a subject to be contacted. "The ground of our being" is a classic example. The huge black block of cast iron that represents God in the "chapel" of the United Nations in New York is the logical end product of this trend. Prayer changes from intercession to meditation. How does one love an It?

This point is not a digression from our theme, for an essential aspect of anthropomorphism in the Bible is that God is almost always described in terms of a man rather than a woman (there are less than ten occasions when he is compared or contrasted with a mother; to treat these as anything other than a comparatively rare exception is to ignore the fact that similar similes are applied to many of the prominent men in the Bible also). When speaking literally of God (rather than metaphorically), the Bible uses the male pronoun without exception. The question therefore arises: Why did God choose to reveal himself in terms of human gender at all and the masculine gender in particular?

Many feminists feel deeply offended by this biblical emphasis, believing that the worship of a "masculine" God (as reflected in our liturgical songs and prayers) is directly responsible for male domination in church and society. Many have already abandoned Christianity as hopelessly identified with this aberration. Others consider it is not too late to bring about a radical shift in theology that could "save" Christianity from extinction in the modern "liberated" world. Their proposed change takes two forms.

One is to think of God as *bisexual*. He combines in his own being the perfection of both masculine and feminine qualities ("male and female" in Genesis 1:27 refers to his "split image," divided between the sexes). To be strictly accurate, I should not have said "he" or "his" in the previous sentence. God must be understood and addressed as our Father-Mother. The Inclusive Language Lectionary of the American National Council of Churches is the first major attempt to incorporate this into a revised version of the Scriptures (it was this publication that prompted one newspaper reviewer to comment, "The devil must be laughing her head off!"). Apart from the practical difficulty of constantly talking about "He-She" and "Him-Her" (only extreme feminists would limit it to "She" and "Her"), this mode of speech plays havoc with our understanding of the Trinity, requiring as it does the incorporation of a mother-daughter relationship into the Godhead (Jesus is now the "Child of God" rather than the "Son of God," "the Human One" rather than the "Son of man").

However, an increasing number of feminist theologians realize that this approach still attributes sexuality to God (even in a bisexual form) and are proposing an alternative solution: that is, to think of God as *asexual*. This approach is certainly more logical. If God is spirit, he is not sexual at all. He is neither masculine nor feminine—so he cannot possibly be both. We must therefore remove all sexual language, not just the "sexist," from Scripture. But what can we put in its place? If we cannot use "He" or "She," the only alternative is "It" language. But this suffers from the same handicap as the rejection of anthropomorphic terms. God becomes so impersonal, so intangible, so unimaginable.

Theological language is then barely distinguishable from the mysticism of the East or the pantheism now pervading the West.

Both these suggestions lead us away from the language of the Bible and away from a biblical relationship with the God who is the Father of Israel and the Father of Jesus. Nor do they answer the question why God revealed himself in such masculine terms in both Testaments. We must choose between two possible explanations.

1. *Divine fatherhood was a reflection of patriarchal society.* Because the world in those days was almost universally patriarchal, it was more or less inevitable that God would be portrayed as a father figure. A liberal view would attribute this to human imagination; a conservative view would attribute it to divine revelation. Either way, it is seen as the best way to think of God *in that era*—a meaningful analogy for authority, protection, care, and so on. However, the metaphor is unsuitable for other societies where governmental patterns are different. In a matriarchal community, so the argument implies, men would have thought of God as a mother and God would have revealed herself as such!

But a major problem arises in an egalitarian society like ours, which has lost respect for leadership and authority figures and wants everyone to be raised (reduced?) to the same level. There are fewer and fewer analogies for a person with superior authority (much less, supreme), at least in democratic countries. Does this explain much of our modern familiarity with God in worship, treating him as our peer, with casual informality rather than the awe and reverence of former generations? We could be treading dangerously near the ultimate idolatry of a society creating God in its own image.

2. *Patriarchal society is a reflection of divine fatherhood.* The position we have just considered is the reverse of reality! Paul himself gives us the true picture of "the Father, from whom all fatherhood [the Greek word is *patria*] in heaven and on earth derives its name" (Ephesians 3:14–15). The human depends upon the divine, not vice versa. God is not just *like* a father; he *is* the Father. The degree to which his type of fatherhood is reflected in ours may vary (the more it does, the more problems we create for ourselves and our children), but it remains the original model.

It is nearer the truth to think of God as masculine rather than feminine. This may explain Paul's unusual and asymmetrical statement that the man "is the image and glory of God; but the woman is the glory of man" (1 Corinthians 11:7). Though Genesis 1 reveals that God gave his image to male and female alike, Genesis 2 reveals that man received it in a direct way and woman in a derived way (as 1 Corinthians 11:8–9 goes on to say).

We conclude that both the anthropomorphic and the masculine language of the Bible bring us nearer to an accurate understanding of and relationship with God than any of the proposed alternatives, however congenial these may be to contemporary thought. After all, it was the Spirit of truth who took the word *Abba* from Jewish family culture and put it on gentile lips (Romans 8:15; Galatians 4:6); he has never inspired the spontaneous cry of recognition: "Mommy!" The Hebrew equivalent of "Daddy" certainly marked the fresh intimacy Jesus brought into fellowship with God—but the term has not lost the respect associated with the relationship. It is supremely expressed in the prayer that until recently was happily used by all Christians: "Our Father in heaven, hallowed be your name. . . ." He is, after all, a *holy* Father—indeed, the only one there has ever been. That fact alone tempers a happy familiarity with a healthy fear. We dare to call him "Father."

APPENDIX

THE SUMMARY CHART